"Men judge more from appearances than reality. All men have eyes, but few have the gift of penetration. Everyone sees your exterior, but few can discern what you have in your heart."

—*Machiavelli*, The Prince, *1532*

45 Effective Ways for

HIRING SMART!

How to Predict

Winners and Losers

in the Incredibly Expensive

People-Reading Game

by Dr. Pierre Mornell

Designed by Kit Hinrichs

Illustrations by Regan Dunnick

Ten Speed Press
Berkeley, California

A Kirsty Melville Book

Publisher

Ten Speed Press, P.O. Box 7123, Berkeley, California 94707 www.tenspeed.com

Distributed in Canada by Ten Speed Press Canada, in Australia by Simon & Schuster Australia, in New Zealand by Tandem Press, in South Africa by Real Books, in Southeast Asia by Berkeley Books, and in the United Kingdom and Europe by Airlift Books.

Design

Cover and interior design by Kit Hinrichs/Pentagram

Design Associate Kashka Pregowska-Czerw/Pentagram

Library of Congress Cataloging-in-Publication Data

Mornell, Pierre.

45 effective ways for hiring smart/how to predict winners and losers in the incredibly expensive people-reading game/by Pierre Mornell; illustrations by Regan Dunnick.

p. cm.

Includes bibliographical references.

ISBN 0-89815-972-5

1. Employee selection.   2. Employees-Recruiting.   3. Interviewing.   I. Title

HF5549.5.S38M673 1998

658.3'11-dc21   97-40126

                                                       CIP

First printing 1998

Printed in Singapore

2 3 4 5 6 7 8 9 10—02 01 00 99 98

For my family

Contents

Acknowledgments

I am deeply grateful to those friends whose wise remarks and illustrative stories appear in the book. My special thanks to John Armstrong, Robin Bacci, Sandy Beebe, Jim Bunch, Jack Boland, Robin Bradford, David Brown, Alan Dachs, Craig Duchossois, Leon Farley, Warren Hellman, George Hume, Howard Lester, Larry Mindel, Paul Orfalea, John Osterweis, Harry V. Quadracci, Gary Rogers, Gordon Segal, Milo Shelly, and Larry Stupski.

I also appreciate the many friends who took time from their busy schedules to read previous drafts of this manuscript and offer their suggestions. Any omissions remain mine, but excellent ideas came from John Davis, Gail Darling, Bob Ferchat, Dan Frederickson, Max Messmer, Jr., Peri Minnesota, Tom Norton, Larry Pidgeon, Brian Pidgeon, Bill Sahlman, Jeffrey Stein, Petey Stein, and Ivan Weinberg.

In addition, I am especially indebted to Doris Ober. She read every draft, every line, every word (many times!), and transformed my well-intentioned prose into clear, concise, and complete ideas. No small feat. Doris worked her magic with professional tough-mindedness and unfailing good cheer. She made it look easy. As did Lynne Morin, who typed draft after draft after draft.

Thanks also go to Howard Stevenson and Carol Franco who helped to break a logjam at the perfect time. And to Kirsty Melville at Ten Speed Press and Kit Hinrichs at Pentagram, who can look around corners and see the future, special thanks. As my publisher and editor,

Kirsty saw the book as it was meant to be. As my collaborator, Kit is not only one of America's leading graphic designers, but a good friend, too. Kit also suggested Regan Dunnick, our extraordinary illustrator. Extraordinary, too, were Aaron Wehner and Kashka Pregowska-Czerw. I was lucky to work with them all.

Finally, my family generously contributed their insights to the book. My wife, Linda, read the manuscript several times, as did my children. An editor, actor, and young businessman, they grew up knowing this prejudice of mine: Nothing you do in life, personally or professionally, is more fun or important than reading people like a book.

Legal Note ☞ *The material in this book stems from my experiences from 1982 to 1997. Specific names and companies are used with permission. However, some stories come from the sources listed on pages 214–218. Where no name appears, the story is a composite, and any similarity to an actual organization or person, living or dead, is purely coincidental. In addition, each of the strategies presented in this book are options in the hiring process. Please consult your legal counsel after devising a selection process to ensure that it is in complete compliance with federal, state, and local laws.*

A New System for Hiring

"You can't spend too much time or effort on "hiring smart." The alternative is to manage tough, which is much more time consuming.**"**

—Gary Rogers, Chairman & CEO, Dreyer's Grand Ice Cream

Introduction: A New System for Hiring

Over the past fifteen years, I've been invited by the presidents of companies, large and small, public and private, to help evaluate and select their key people. From the resulting years of trial and error, I've developed an almost fail-safe method for predicting behavior that works for hiring all levels of employees, from entry-level staff to company presidents.

Why is a hiring decision so important? Because of the high cost of mistakes. My rule of thumb is: *If you make a mistake in hiring, and you recognize and rectify the mistake within six months, the cost of replacing that employee is two and one-half times the person's annual salary.*

Put another way, the wrong person earning $50,000 will cost your company $125,000. The wrong executive making $100,000 will cost you a quarter of a million dollars *if you rectify the mistake within six months.* And this economic estimate doesn't even consider the emotional costs. Who among us hasn't driven home or lain awake at night having imaginary conversations with a troubled employee or difficult colleague?

Before an annual seminar I conduct for executives from around the world, I once sent out a nonscientific survey to about one hundred past and present clients. There were just three short questions:

1. **What was your worst hire?**

2. **How long did the situation take to resolve?**

3. **How much did the mistake cost?**

A staggering 70 percent of the executives returned their surveys within one week. And their answers were equally amazing.

How long did it take to resolve the situation?

> Median: **1 year**

> Average: **1.5 years**

How much did the mistake cost?

> Median: **$300,000**

> Average: **$1,087,863**

Comments ranged from "I'll never hire anyone again," to "It cost me the company." As the recruiting director for Microsoft has said, "The best thing we can do for our competitors is to hire poorly."

The lesson is clear. Whether you are a small-business owner, the director of a not-for-profit organization, or the CEO of a Fortune 500 company, success depends upon your ability to hire the right men and women. People are our most valuable assets.

Yet the top ten business schools offer no ongoing courses about how to evaluate, select, or hire key people. In fact, MBA students today are offered courses about the opposite—how to get themselves hired by performing well in interviews. For example, Duke University has a required course in "Individual Effectiveness," partly devoted to interviewing skills, job-offer negotiations, telephone etiquette, and other tips for the applicant. A required career management seminar series at NYU's graduate school of business includes "How to Work a Room." I have written this book from a rather different perspective, inspired by a man who was a master at predicting winners—the San Francisco 49ers' chief scout Tony Razzano.

During the 1980s the 49ers won four Super Bowls. They were professional football's best team and were hailed as the "Team of the Decade." One reason for their great success was Tony Razzano's selection system.

The system was no secret; it had proven itself after he made a mistake in selecting a punter, Jim Miller. In an empty stadium, Razzano had watched Miller boom ten kicks with his shoe on and ten kicks with his shoe off. He looked like Superman. Based on Miller's performance that day, Razzano had recommended he be drafted as the 49ers' next punter. "I thought that was a no-miss thing," Razzano said.

But faced with the realities of crowds, wind, bungled snaps, and the oncoming rush of 300-pound defensive linemen, Jim Miller apparently couldn't handle the pressure. After three inconsistent seasons, the 49ers cut him. It turned out to be a watershed—if expensive—lesson for Tony Razzano. The 49ers had deviated from their selection system and paid the price.

After Miller, Razzano insisted on observing a player *in action* for at least 200 plays. "I like studying over 200 plays. When you see that many plays, you have a feel for what a player can and can't do," he said.

Using Razzano's system, the San Francisco 49ers picked Joe Montana in the third round of the NFL draft. Montana was the eighty-second player taken that year. Jerry Rice was selected using a similar method and was the sixteenth player taken in his draft. Montana became a quarterbacking legend, leading the 49ers to those four Super Bowl titles. Rice, shunned by more than a dozen teams in the draft, is widely considered the best receiver ever to play the game.

The other twenty-seven NFL teams selected their players primarily from the workouts of potential pro players in the league's annual meat market for college players. By invitation, these athletes perform before scouts in an otherwise unoccupied football stadium, demonstrating their individual skills in such events as the forty-yard dash, bench press, and vertical jump—but the stadium is empty. Tony Razzano said, *"200 plays."* He meant real live situations.

Of course, you're rarely going to see 200 demonstrations of a candidate's talent before you make a decision. But you can see twenty such moves—before, during, and after the interview. You can also hear about another twenty actions or reactions in various contexts from people who know the candidate on and off the record. That's about forty snapshots of a person's behavior. Watching a person respond to forty or even twenty challenges, you're less likely to be dazzled by a single shining interview, or to be influenced by a strong first impression. *And the less likely you are to hire the next warm body who walks into your office.*

In this book I suggest forty-five strategies designed to take the measure of an applicant. My suggestions are not hard-and-fast rules. They are opportunities to improve your hiring tools. They are the basis of a new selection system that will take you considerably less time than hours of interviews by emphasizing behavior, not words.

The system affirms Mornell's Maxim, which says, "The best predictor of future behavior is past behavior." It's a conclusion based on thirty years of psychiatric experience in which I have seen not only a person's exterior, but what that person holds inside. Neither optimistic nor pessimistic, Mornell's Maxim represents reality as I see it. If a woman was a Type A personality yesterday, with all of its advantages and disadvantages, you can bet on her being a Type A tomorrow. If a man was great with people but lousy with details in his last three jobs, you can predict his future behavior accordingly. If control was an important issue last year, it will be this year.

Mornell's Maxim applies to more than just hiring job applicants. Several years ago I spoke in Istanbul at an international conference of 500 company presidents. After I finished speaking about "Picking Winners by Hiring Smart," I wandered down the hall to where another speaker had just started his lecture. His name was Herb Cohen, the author of *You Can Negotiate Anything*, and he was expounding about an overhead projection slide that read, "There's a cardinal rule in negotiations. The best predictor of a person's future negotiating behavior is his past negotiating behavior."

Although Herb Cohen and I had never met, nor had he heard my lecture, within an hour of each other's talks in a conference center in Turkey, we were both teaching the same lesson: Negotiating or hiring, the more we know about the person across the table, the better our predictive powers and the fewer our surprises.

Of course, there are exceptions. Ray Kroc was, at best, an average salesman until his early fifties. Then he discovered how to mass merchandise hamburgers and founded McDonald's. He may have been highly entrepreneurial at a very young age, but he never excelled in more structured environments.

The lesson is critical. *Everyone* makes mistakes in their career, and sometimes bad things (or bad bosses) happen to good people. It's important to recognize these human realities, and to discuss them as part of the hiring process.

So what I've compiled here are clearly more than interview skills. In fact, the pre-interview–strategies section of the book is designed to eliminate up to 80 percent of inappropriate applicants, thus reducing the need for any interview at all.

In addition, I am interested in making a good match, not in tricking candidates into revealing their weaknesses. In business, as in everything else, weaknesses are as much a fact of life as strengths. So this book considers a candidate's past, present, and future as it might relate to the hiring company now and in the long term.

For clarity, I've divided the book's next five sections into strategies you might adopt or adapt for your own hiring system before the interview, during the interview, and after the interview, followed by tips for checking references and some final strategies. Most of the strategies I'll present will help you evaluate how a candidate performs. However, some suggestions are included in order to elicit more information from a candidate and to make the interviewing process more enjoyable. I've also included a variety of practical information on pages 185–213 that I hope you will find helpful.

I have three goals. First, I want to demonstrate *a practical and efficient method for evaluating people* that will lead to more accurate predictions of their behavior. Some methods, such as meeting the spouse, apply more to senior executives than entry-level staff, but you can adapt these strategies accordingly. Second, I hope that you will take away *at least three new ideas about hiring* key people. Third, as a result, I trust that you will *save significant time, energy, and money* in your next hire.

That's what this book is all about.

Contents: Chapter 1

Pre-Interview Strategies

"If you're wise in the choice of your partners, you'll do very well, and, similarly, if you're wise in your selection of businesses and people to run them, you'll prosper. Pretty much, the rest doesn't count."

—Warren Hellman, Investor

Chapter 1: Pre-Interview Strategies

Most interviewees prepare their strategy in advance for what, inevitably, is a predictable series of interview steps. The candidates can prepare an excellent resume. And should. The candidates can anticipate questions and practice their answers. And should. The company can and should prepare by rethinking the job and redefining the position, including the critical skills and ideal person necessary to perform the job.

In addition, if you script a few additional *pre-interview* plays, your evaluation begins long before the hiring game officially starts. You've developed a strategy for which there can be little preparation by the candidate in advance of your meeting. A less predictable interview allows you more accurately to evaluate how he or she will actually perform on the job.

And this is crucial to more than just future performance. You're about to begin a long-term relationship with the person you hire. For better or worse, you're considering a potential marriage. It's a two-way street, and it's in everybody's interest to be both diplomatic *and* candid whenever you anticipate a long-term relationship.

For example, I interviewed four editors who were interested in this book: two in New York, one in Boston, one in Northern California. Knowing that my editor and I would have to work together for the better part of a year (and if all went well, on other projects in the future), the interview cut two ways. The editors looked at me. And I looked at them.

Thinking about a long-term relationship is very different than thinking about trick questions and body language in an interview. Your purpose is not to trip up the person, but to make the best possible match. So here are several suggestions that can provide information about a candidate before the interview formally begins.

Strategy No. 1:

Make Phone Contact with the Candidate

Before the initial interview, pick up the phone and call the candidate. Whether you're the president of a company interviewing your prospective assistant or the manager of an ad agency interviewing an incoming creative talent, place the phone call yourself.

How hard or easy is it to reach the candidate? Does the candidate return your call at the specific times that you suggest? Is she an articulate communicator in your conversation? What else can you tell about the candidate in the first two minutes? Paradoxically, some good candidates are uncomfortable on the phone, whereas most con men have a terrific phone presence. So unless you're hiring a telephone receptionist, consider this information as only one piece in a 200-piece puzzle. However, should you call shortly after lunch and learn that the candidate must be awakened from a deep sleep (a true story), assuming he doesn't work the night shift at Lockheed, you're probably looking at a red light.

I review time, place, and dress for the initial interview by phone. I say something like, "If you're available at 11:00 A.M. next Tuesday, I'll send directions to my office. I know you're coming by car (or plane), so please dress comfortably. Do you have any questions? If not, we'll see you at 11:00 next Tuesday."

Why is personal contact for two minutes such a simple, effective predictor of future behavior? Here's an example.

Several years ago, a friend from New York asked me to interview an executive candidate who ran a large division for a Fortune 500 company. As the candidate's previous interviews in New York had been outstanding, I asked my friend what he wanted me to look for when I met the man in California. He said, "Is the candidate flexible? Can he shift gears from a large corporation to an entrepreneurial enterprise in New York? He's used to being in charge. Will he give up control to work under me? For that matter, can I give up control to him?"

I called the candidate and went through my two-minute phone call. The candidate asked for directions via fax, adding that he knew San Francisco because his sister lived in San Jose. Brief, yes. Simple, definitely. Time consuming, not. So what happened?

The candidate did not arrive at the agreed upon hour, say, 11:00 A.M. Nor did he arrive at 11:15. Noon came and went. Still no candidate. No phone call. No fax. Nothing until 12:30 P.M.

One hour and thirty minutes after our scheduled interview, there was a knock on my door. Relieved that the candidate had finally found the office, I opened the door to find a man dressed in a three-piece, dark blue suit, starched white shirt, red power tie, and highly polished black oxford shoes. He said, "Goddamn San Francisco!" Literally, these were Mr. Fortune 500's first three words.

It turned out that he had not followed my directions. "Knowing San Francisco" from his previous trips to his sister's San Jose house, the candidate disregarded my map and tried to come north through San Francisco on a freeway that, unfortunately, had been leveled by the '89 earthquake.

Now, we've all had trouble finding a new office. We've all been delayed by a hotel operator's late wake-up call, or a cab driver's wrong turn. Yet there are telephones in San Francisco. At the nearest telephone, we would have stopped, called, and reported our whereabouts. We would have said something like "Sorry, I know it's 10:45 (or 11:00 or even 11:15), but the rental car has a flat tire;" or "The cab driver has made a wrong turn. I'm terribly sorry for the inconvenience. Will you still be there in thirty minutes?"

The New York candidate had been in my office for less than five seconds. And yet I had already discovered that he disregarded directions. Contrary to my instructions about comfortable clothes, he was wearing a three-piece suit—but maybe that was his idea of comfortable. In any case, he was not flexible enough to deviate from his rigid routine of driving to the Golden Gate Bridge. So standing at the front door, five seconds into our time together, I was ready to show the candidate the way back to San Jose or, better yet, put him on the plane back home.

With a six-figure salary riding on the outcome of our interview, the fat lady had already sung.

It's not that the New York candidate got lost in San Francisco. It's his behavior. Mr. Fortune 500 blames his personal shortcomings on "goddamn San Francisco." Although I probably should have said my next appointment was at 1:00, even if the candidate had come 2,500 miles, I didn't end the interview, and we spent the next two hours discussing the man's career. Whereas he might have been a good manager at a large corporation, and maybe even gotten results from his people, he was not the candidate for my friend in New York. As far as I could see, his series of successful interviews at the home office were like Jim Miller's twenty punts in an empty stadium. Impressive, but misleading.

How typical is this story? Five to 10 percent of interviewees will screw up this first test. If they do, you should consider their behavior a *flashing red light. Stop. And proceed at your own risk.*

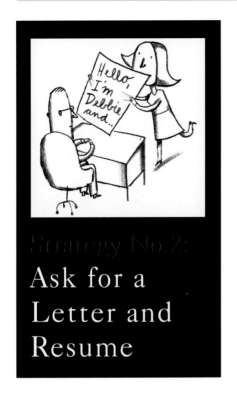

Strategy No. 2:

Ask for a Letter and Resume

If appropriate, regardless of the material already in your file, ask the candidate to send a resume with a one-page cover letter that briefly highlights his or her life and background. This can be requested in your initial phone call.

This request provides the following information: Is the response slow or prompt? How long before the letter and resume arrive by mail or fax? Is the candidate literate or illiterate? Sloppy or neat? When I was looking for a detail-oriented secretary, one applicant wrote, "I was *excepted* to UC Berkeley." As you can imagine, I saved myself an interview.

Here are some sobering realities about resumes. Microsoft gets about 12,000 resumes a month. Every one is logged into a computer, noting time and date of arrival, the reader's reactions, and the date of Microsoft's response. The company devotes an enormous amount of time to reading these resumes. But Microsoft thinks it's worthwhile, because the company believes that "Our best asset is our intellectual horsepower."

Yet there's another set of realities about resumes. Ward Howell's executive search firm once estimated that 65 percent of executive candidates lie about their academic credentials. Forty-three percent lie about their job responsibilities. Forty-two percent lie about previous compensation. Clearly some of the best fiction being written today is on resumes. And it's not only executives.

A recent review of medical students' fellowship applications by the University of Pittsburgh School of Medicine found that 29 to 35 percent lied about their research, presentations, and articles. The reason cited by the researchers: intense competition.

In addition, in a recent survey of 6,000 students, seventy percent of undergraduate students in the United States admitted to cheating on exams. It is a "significant increase" over previous years, according to Donald McCabe of Rutgers University, who headed the survey team. And McCabe added, "Their logic? Everyone's doing it, or so students told me."

Given these realities, a resume must always be verified. For example, let's say that you're interested in a candidate. He's perfect. Yet you know a high percentage of people fudge on their college credentials, and that young people are fudging in record numbers. Whether it's due to intense competition, or the attitude that "everybody's doing it," you can check a candidate's resume even before the interview, if you choose. Here's what a friend discovered when he made this effort: ☞

Dear Pierre,

Recently, we were interviewing candidates for a lower level, but rather important, administrative position. One young man struck us as particularly attractive. He was bright, articulate, and very interested in our business. He had some directly applicable work experience and a fair amount of fascinating other work experience. In short, we thought we had found someone who could do the job at hand, and possibly grow well beyond.

Some little voice, perhaps yours, told me that we needed to get a more factual picture. The risk was that our candidate might be too good to be true. Listening to this little voice, we therefore called Vanderbilt University to ascertain our candidate's degree.

Lo and behold, the Bachelor of Arts in English Literature with a 3.5 GPA was not to be found. Our candidate had attended, but not, as it turned out, graduated from Vanderbilt. Needless to say, we allowed him to pursue his job search elsewhere, where personal integrity is not the sine qua non that it is in our business.

Your insistence on getting facts related to a candidate's past performance clearly proved invaluable in this instance. Thanks again!

My friend Milo Shelly, who for seventeen years was the human resource director with the Ernest and Julio Gallo Winery, tells a story about resume reading that should be a lesson to us all. "Early in my career, I received the resume of a sales applicant from a headhunter stating what a great guy he was. He 'fit our specs to a tee.' In reviewing the resume, I noticed a four-year gap. One might have thought it was an omission, or perhaps the individual had spent time in the military. Turns out the applicant murdered his wife and did time. Maybe I should have been more understanding—it was only third-degree murder!"

Resumes can also reveal less dramatic problems. Here's an example.

After interviewing a candidate, a client sent me the fellow's resume. Coincidentally, the candidate was someone I had interviewed several years earlier for a company in Los Angeles. Scanning his resume, I noticed that he had buried his year-long employment with that company deep in a long list of independent consulting jobs. Unless a reference checker was extremely compulsive, there was no way to know that the candidate had falsified his resume...unless I said something, which I did.

When the client asked the candidate about the discrepancy, he came clean. He had worked as an independent consultant as part of his termination agreement with the company, so that part was true. However, the candidate had been guilty by omission and he immediately submitted a corrected chronology of his work history.

The question is: What would you do in this situation?

My own perspective is rather simple. If the candidate had said earlier in the selection process, "Several years ago I had a disastrous relationship with a difficult boss whom I haven't listed on my resume. He was the only employer I ever had trouble with, but if you want his name or the details, I'll provide them," I would have understood. We all make mistakes, learn from our so-called failures, and go on. But the candidate didn't do that. Instead, he joined the 43 percent of executives who lie about previous job responsibilities on their resume.

I think that it is a red light if a person behaves deceptively on something as basic as a resume. This is a rather uncompromising position, but in the few cases where I've ignored this principle, the candidate has burned the future employer. Whenever I've trusted the rule, an excellent candidate has eventually emerged, although the hiring process may have taken a little longer.

Give an Assignment Before the Interview

Ask the candidate to visit one of your stores, plants, campuses, offices, or Web page before the interview. Then ask for the candidate's observations.

As with the one-page letter and resume, this requirement asks for a demonstration of how a person carries out an actual task. For example, say I'm the marketing director of a small chain of Italian white-tablecloth restaurants. If a potential employee has already visited a location before an interview and can offer some insights about the restaurant's food and service, location, design, and cleanliness, I'd say that particular candidate has spoken volumes before the interview. Furthermore, some retail store owners have told me that if a candidate has never visited their establishment with or without such an assignment, it's a definite nix on hiring.

Okay, a reality check before you read further. Let's agree that this test requires that candidates rave about your shop, stores, plants, or restaurants. But what else do they say? Is it insightful, helpful, specific, and accurate? Does the candidate see problems, suggest solutions?

For example, at the end of a day's seminar for American Golf Corporation, which operates more than 250 golf courses in North America and Europe, the management committee decided that all their potential employees, including hourly workers, would be required to visit one of their golf courses before the interview. They'd then be asked to comment on the course's overall condition, the cleanliness of the clubhouse, the ease of obtaining starting times, the food and beverage facilities, as well as customer service. This was one of three or four take-home ideas at our seminar—one that effectively shifts the 800-pound hiring gorilla from the interviewer to the interviewee.

Following our seminar, a twenty-seven-year-old candidate wrote a four-page report before his initial interview, which included an evaluation of concessions, bar and restaurant, catering, management team, course quality, and pro shop. On the following page is an example from the beginning of his report. ☛

Thoughts on Concessions

- 5.5 oz pretzels are popular, retailing for $1.50
  and a COS (Cost of Sale) of 16%-20%.

- Adding chili and/or cheese to items for 75 cents
  is a great addition. Low COS and adds value.

- Ice cream products and novelties could be a big
  seller. Even hand-dipped ice cream would be possible with a low COS and a higher perceived value.

- Hand foods like hot dogs on a stick, cheese sticks,
  icees, milk shakes, cotton candy, popcorn, frozen
  lemonade, mini burritos, taquitos, onion rings,
  and souvenir cups with refill program are some of
  the ideas that use similar preparation equipment,
  have good holding abilities, and great COS.

- Upsell portions are a creative way to add value
  and increase gross sales.

  - Larger sodas for 16 oz, 24 oz large,
    32 oz jumbo.

  - Double your order for a "buck." Wendy's,
    McDonald's, Jack in the Box, and airport
    bars use this to increase gross sales
    (french fries, burgers, and beverages).

- Insert visual displays into the menu board to help increase sales. People buy only what they can visualize.

- Menu board is somewhat confusing; better use of lettering for easy focus.

- The breakfast menu could be a separate menu brought out in the morning and replaced by the lunch staff closer to noon. This would help to simplify and specialize.

- Display more impulse items in the window (i.e., pretzels, cookies, candy, etc.).

- Pricing appears to be in the right range; however, here are a few thoughts.

  - The standard hot dog pricing is a bit high.

  - Soda pricing could be increased. You could even add a refill program to increase value.

  - Of course, COS is critical. Purchasing, waste, and theft would need to be examined to make an overall judgment. However, COS needs to be running in the 28% range for these products.

Obviously it was an extraordinarily detailed report, and it impressed the interviewer. Furthermore, the candidate's specific suggestions were practical. In fact, American Golf immediately implemented them.

Here's another example from a bank in upstate New York. Laura Marcantonio is Executive Vice President of Herkimer Country Trust Company (HCT), established in 1833 in Little Falls, New York. Before interviewing finalist candidates—prospective assistants—she asked each to visit a branch office and to mail or fax a report about how their services and operations appeared. She did not offer any guidelines. When she received the report she would then schedule an interview.

On the right is the summary from one candidate's report. ☞

Summary

Overall I was very pleased with the atmosphere, friendliness, and accommodation that was provided by the Herkimer branch. My first impression is that HCT offers the personal interaction required to make their customers feel HCT is working with them and for them and will make every effort to meet the customer's needs.

However, I felt there were two ways the first experience of a new or potential customer could be improved. The first would be to clearly indicate one person or area in the bank that a new or potential customer could easily identify and approach, without hesitation, with any questions.

I also feel it would be beneficial if HCT provided a brochure that gave a complete listing of all the services provided. Sharon was very helpful in providing brochures regarding checking, savings, loans, credit cards, mortgage options, ready reserve, and rate schedules. However, as a potential customer, I would have preferred one brochure that gave me an overview of all of HCT's services. This would allow me to see at a glance which services HCT could provide that are comparable to the services I am now receiving at other banks. It would also provide information as to what additional options are available that I may not know about, and therefore may not think to ask about.

Not all assignments achieve such positive results, and such insightful, in-depth reports are rare. However, both the bank and golf candidates also interviewed extremely well. They did not give the impression that they would want to come in and change everything before getting to know operations more intimately. Their references were outstanding, and the results of twenty more demonstrations of their behavior were equally impressive. They were both hired.

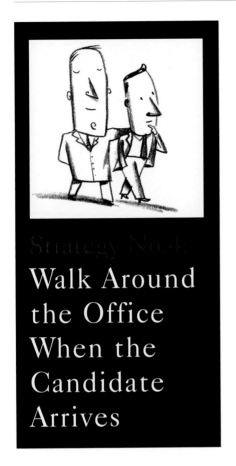

Strategy No. 4:

Walk Around the Office When the Candidate Arrives

Most candidates wait for the beginning of the "official" interview like a runner waits for the starter's gun to fire. These few minutes are a terrific opportunity to take a brief stroll about the office and make small talk, while lowering anxieties. "How was your drive? Any trouble finding the office? Would you like some coffee?" Look for curiosity—does the candidate ask questions? What other behavior does the candidate exhibit?

My office is a remodeled 1890s house in Mill Valley, California. In the front yard stands a hundred-year-old ponderosa pine. In the living room, which serves as my office, there are pictures of my wife riding a horse, our son at his college graduation, and our two daughters on Outward Bound rafting and backpacking trips. Adjacent is a small conference room with floor-to-ceiling bookshelves and several hundred books. Lining the walls are mementos from my travels in Africa, Asia, and the Middle East, along with large two-foot-by-four-foot photos of wilderness areas in Montana, Oregon, and California from my days as a founding director of a land conservancy.

Why do I mention the house and photographs?

Let's say that a client calls and asks me to interview a candidate. One of the things he usually wants to know is, "Is the candidate curious?" Curiosity is a valuable asset in an employee. It demonstrates a desire to gratify the mind with new discoveries, to learn about novel and extraordinary things. Curiosity augurs well for a candidate's success, especially in entrepreneurial enterprises. And my office provides candidates the opportunity to show their curiosity. Interestingly, the candidate who knows that I am a psychiatrist beforehand is usually nervous. Nervousness, in turn, can lead to an invisible wall between us—call it shyness or fear—which can result in a reluctance to ask questions, at least in the initial hour of most interviews. However, about 10 percent never ask questions at all. There's apparently no curiosity or interest in the house, garden, or jumble of personal items inside the office, which surely tells more about me and my family than I could ever put in words.

To be fair, these candidates do ask questions about the job once the interview is over. About the organization. About the compensation. About the personality fit between themselves and the culture. Good questions. But when not one comment is made or question asked about any of the rather unique clutter amidst which the candidate is sitting, I have a sense in a preliminary way about that person's curiosity level—or at least as it expresses itself in my office.

Let me tell a story about Gordon and Carole Segal, who started Crate and Barrel as a single store about thirty-five years ago on the north side of Chicago. A smashing success, Crate and Barrel now has more than seventy stores throughout the United States. One day Gordon called and said, "Pierre, I have a great candidate to be my chief operating officer, but he's a financial guy. What questions should I ask to find out about his people skills?" Spontaneously, I said, "Forget the questions, Gordon. You're an expert with people. Walk around with the fellow. You'll see him in action, even if it's admittedly an artificial situation and he's on his best behavior. Get out of your office before the interview officially starts, and see how the candidate reacts to the people he meets. You'll have your answer within a few minutes."

I know Gordon's office. Not only do Crate and Barrel's executive offices adjoin dozens of staff and secretarial spaces—they adjoin warehouse space, too. Everyone works within spitting distance of everyone else. Best behavior aside, is the candidate more comfortable with executives? Secretaries? Warehouse people? What's their first impression of him? What else can we predict from the candidate's walkabout?

In this case, Gordon loved the candidate. His people skills, past and present, were terrific, especially for a financial wizard. So after a three-month evaluation and courtship, which involved the candidate and his family—let's say 30 plays later—Gordon did a "trial close." He said, "What would it take to bring you to Chicago?" And the candidate answered. Afterwards, Gordon offered him a job. Ironically, the candidate turned him down. Using the leverage of his Crate and Barrel offer, the candidate apparently increased his salary handsomely with his current employer in New York, despite Gordon Segal's best efforts on Crate and Barrel's behalf.

Did Gordon predict the eventual outcome? No. Was the walkabout worth it? Sure. Was the walkabout a better predictor of people skills than Gordon's interview questions in a confined office space? You bet. Besides, it's infinitely more fun to walk around your office, or my office, or Gordon's office, than to sweat bullets conducting lengthy interviews when this pre-interview strategy is available.

Strategy No.5:
Read Resumes in Teams If Possible

It's helpful—and faster—to read the top candidates' resumes in teams of three to five people. Watch for one of your team members to emerge, often unpredictably, as your in-house resume expert. Teams add vitality to the entire evaluation process, not only to the reading of resumes. (See also Strategy 21, Interview in Teams, page 88). Why teams? Because teams that work well together are more accurate and insightful about potential employees than individuals are.

For example, here's a section of a twenty-seven-year-old graduate student's resume. He was applying for a marketing position during an upcoming four-month summer internship with a marketing company. ☛

Education

1995–1997   **Harvard University Graduate School
             of Business Administration**   **Boston, MA**
             Candidate for Master in Business Administration degree,
             June 1997. Active in Asian Business Club.

1986–1990   **University of California, Berkeley**   **Berkeley, CA**
             Awarded Bachelor of Arts degree, cum laude, in history, 1990. Varsity
             men's lacrosse team four years, elected Team President in 1989 and
             received *Most Inspirational Player Award* in 1990.

Experience

1992–1995   **Nissho Iwai**   **Tokyo, Japan**
             Marketing Manager. Directed new projects, consumer research, and
             marketing strategies for penetration of the Japanese market. Joint venture
             (30 employees) between one of Japan's largest trading companies,
             Nissho Iwai, and an American manufacturer. Sole "gaijin" (foreigner) in
             the company.
             • Directed five new product launches in all stages of development,
               from consumer focus groups through product advertising. New
               product introduction increased sales revenue by $10 million.
             • Managed $250,000 R&D budget with emphasis on Japanese
               consumer preferences for product categories. Co-managed $5 million
               advertising budget.
             • Developed seminars by invitation for Nissho Iwai international forums.
               Presented to a group of European managers training in Tokyo in
               association with Japan's Ministry of International Industry and Trade
               (MITI). Topics included consumer product penetration of the
               Japanese market focusing on marketing and distribution.

1990–1991   **Gymespace Vit'Halles**   **Paris, France**
             Personal Trainer/Professor d'Musculation.
             Operated an independent business.
             • Worked with private clientele.
             • Taught various health classes exclusively in French.

1989   **United States Senate,
             Office of Senator Herb Kohl**   **Washington, DC**
             Aide on the Judiciary Committee. Assisted Senator's Chief Counsel on
             pending legislation before the Judiciary Committee.
             • Briefed Senator Kohl and staff on variety of issues, culminating in
               extensive research and drafting of the Senator's speech regarding the
               impeachment of Judge Alcee Hastings.
             • Performed legislative research on gun control, cable television, and
               Chinese student immigration policies.
             • Responded to constituent inquiries and carried out diverse
               administrative responsibilities.

             Languages: *French and Japanese*

Most interviewers and recruiters scan the resume and notice three items:

1.   He's at Harvard Business School.

2.   He speaks Japanese and French.

3.   He's traveled extensively.

When a group of people went over the candidate's resume they thought that his global experiences and Japanese proficiency were impressive items. But was there a gap in 1991–92 between France and Japan? Good question. It turns out he was unemployed for nine months. Then he directed product launches and developed international seminars. But who did the young man lead, or manage? One member thought the candidate's resume defined him as a risk-taker, a positive. But another reader saw it as a negative, too unfocused for a twenty-seven-year-old. A third member of the resume team knew Japan, and how rare and hard it was for a foreigner to adapt in a traditional Japanese company. The discussion was quick and more complete than if a single reader had reviewed the candidate's credentials.

Of course there's another perspective. Teams can also waste time and pass over good candidates if the group feels "we *must* have consensus," or if a dominant member monopolizes the discussion. On the other hand, when teams work well together, it assures a depth of reading you're less likely to achieve on your own.

PS: The marketing firm decided to take a chance with the recruit and offered him the summer internship.

Strategy No.6:

Cast the Widest Net Possible

All these pre-interview strategies assume the best possible choices. But these choices can only be as good as the candidate pool you attract. With a better quality of people participating in the application process, you're sure to have better finalists. How can you raise the bar and find better candidates?

Let a wide range of people know that you're looking for better candidates: friends, colleagues, consultants, professional associates, board members, ex-employees, even family members, as well as search firms and trade groups. You can use services on the Internet and call college career centers. You can create your own Web site. (Cisco Systems' Web site has a jobs page that records up to 500,000 visits per month!) Clearly, the wider net you cast, the more likely you are to catch the big fish. In addition, you might keep data banks of excellent candidates who elect to work elsewhere. Call them. Who do they know? On occasion, they'll even suggest themselves.

You also need to recognize excellent people wherever you find them. Sometimes you find them by casting the widest net possible. Other times you find them by casting to attract a specific person.

For example, I evaluated a financial whiz who was working for Toyota in Los Angeles after having graduated from the Anderson School of Business at UCLA. Dave Pillsbury of American Golf Corporation wanted this young man to change jobs, shift careers, and become his eventual successor. Dave asked me what I thought. Would I recommend the fellow?

Dave had found this candidate at a party, of all places. Sitting across from him for over two hours at a dinner table, Dave had observed that he interacted easily, even brilliantly, with a variety of men and women in a social setting. Within twenty-four hours Dave had called him and said, "Can you meet with me to discuss a business proposal?"

He had previously spotted an assistant manager behind the desk at an Embassy Suites hotel outside of St. Louis. Dealing with a difficult customer ahead of Dave in line, the assistant manager had listened with endless patience to the guest's complaint, dealt with the problem, and resolved a potential crisis to everyone's satisfaction. Dave asked him for a meeting. The man, just age 31, now runs a multimillion-dollar country club in Bel Air, California.

What Dave observed at the dinner party and hotel were the potential candidates' behaviors. Casting the widest net possible, he is *always* on the lookout for the best candidates available, and he usually finds them.

The story is not unusual. Microsoft maintains its own internal "Strike Team in Recruiting," a staff that phones potential leads around the country from six in the morning until eight at night. Microsoft assumes that the best candidates are not looking for new jobs. In fact, candidates who approach Microsoft are actually less attractive to the company.

How important are great players to Microsoft? As Bill Gates has said, "Take our twenty best people away, and I will tell you that we would become an unimportant company."

Use Caution Around Any Big Changes

Hiring people from big companies to little companies, top-down to bottom-up organizations, or structured to entrepreneurial settings, can be a dangerous route. You don't ask an Olympic sprinter in the 100 meters to compete in the mile run. Nor do you think about using a 300-pound defensive tackle as your team's quarterback. So it is that a successful executive from retail grocery stores may have trouble steering a shipping company, a litigation attorney is often out of his comfort zone running a low-key, not-for-profit organization, and retired IBM managers seldom do well as hedge fund investors. Begin your search focused on the talent within your industry, culture, or business, or on less experienced talent within your organization, before you start searching elsewhere.

Of course we all know of exceptions. So keep them in mind too as you consider this strategy.

Rethink the Position Before the Interview

Before interviewing new candidates for old jobs, it's an excellent time to rethink the job itself.

This suggestion is really a pre-pre-interview tip, like Cast the Widest Net Possible. Let's say that the last creative director of an ad agency was a genius at copywriting, but couldn't administer his department or handle details. If you can afford the luxury, why not split the job? One person acts as the right brain—the creative leader. The other person acts as the left brain—the logical administrative whiz. If you redefine the position and create two well-defined jobs, the creative director need not worry about details and organization. Instead, the director is free to worry about thirty-second ad campaigns that please clients and sell products.

For example, several years ago I took partners from one of the world's leading design firms, Pentagram, on a three-day retreat to Sedona, Arizona. Pentagram partners are visual, innovative, creative, idiosyncratic, eccentric, right-brain, brilliant designers. However, a three-day event that brings in people from London, New York, and San Francisco to Sedona, Arizona, requires airline tickets, airport transportation, hotel reservations, meal arrangements, plus audiovisual requirements, such as VCRs, TV monitors, flip charts, marking pens, overhead projectors, slide projectors, pointers, pads, pens, and retreat handouts, plus coordinating such details as coffee breaks and dinner reservations. That's why the partners asked an office administrator to work with me in advance of the Sedona retreat to ensure that the logistics would be smooth, inconspicuous, and perfect in Arizona. And they were.

Like many artists, most Pentagram partners would have trouble organizing a two-car funeral. They have almost no left brain. So when it became financially feasible to add an extra employee, it didn't take Pentagram partners long to rethink the "artist as administrator" job and split the duties by hiring an office manager.

There's a contrary viewpoint, of course. While rethinking the position, you might discover the job isn't necessary. You can eliminate paperwork, duplication, overhead, and insurance, plus save yourself a lot of time and money by doing away with the position entirely. That's happened in this decade, and many businesses have taken advantage of this rationale. Using euphemisms like downsizing and reengineering, corporations have cut the fat, and sometimes the muscle, of their organizations.

However, "Rethink the Position" is *not* synonymous with using a meat ax when a scalpel will do. It is synonymous with the questions: Can the position be streamlined? Can the person be utilized in a more effective manner? This requires as clearsighted a consideration of the job as you expect to bestow on the candidate.

Strategy No.9:

Use Pre-Interview Tips in Combinations

Whether you expect eight or 800 resumes, integrating several of the preceding strategies into your hiring system will eventually save you a lot of time.

Like so many office manager ads, this one was generic:

ADMINISTRATIVE ASSISTANT/ OFFICE MANAGER:

Full time. Fun. Fast-paced, not-for-profit organization working with high-potential/ low-income high school students, seeks organized/flexible person with strong work ethic & values/written & oral communication skills/sense of humor. Grant-writing experience helpful. Mac computer skills a must. Salary competitive. Send resume and one page cover letter to...

Before placing the ad, the organization had adapted four pre-interview strategies from the pages you have just read. Deciding *which* four took some time, but at the end, everyone agreed it was time well spent. This is what they used: ☛

1. Cast the Widest Net Possible

The organization's three-person staff asked their friends and acquaintances for potential candidates. Who did they know? Who would they recommend? This strategy produced two candidates.

Within two weeks the ad had produced seventy-eight resumes, and the pool of applicants reached eighty.

2. Ask for a Cover Letter

Although candidates did not know the salary, they did know to send a cover letter. Twenty percent of the candidates were eliminated immediately because their resumes arrived without a cover letter, and another ten percent arrived with handwritten notes. One such note included this unasked-for piece of information: "I wake up at 5:00 A.M. each morning to work on my spiritual, mental, and fiscal health." Maybe this applicant knew something that the not-for-profit didn't, but he was eliminated because the organization was serious about finding a perfectionist with strong written communication skills. No cover letter, or a weak cover letter, and no next step.

3. Read Resumes in Teams

Normally, it would take the executive director several days to plow through the fifty-six remaining resumes. And reading resumes can be about as much fun as watching paint dry. So team resume reading was a great time-saver for the organization, cutting the pre-interview resume reading time down to half-a-day's work.

The team funneled resumes into one of three stacks. In Pile A were candidates who would definitely get a phone call in return for their intelligent letters and interesting resumes. In Pile B were the maybes. And Pile C contained the rest—all the resumes with misspellings and typos. Also in Pile C were resumes from candidates who simply weren't qualified, about thirty percent of the total. This process left fifteen applications in Pile A.

4. Make Phone Contact with the Applicants in Pile A

The phone calls took less than five minutes per applicant. The hiring team then answered the following questions about each candidate: 1) How hard or easy was it to reach the applicant? 2) How good were the applicant's phone skills? Every candidate who passed was asked to come for an initial interview.

The organization soon discovered that some candidates could write a great cover letter and some had a terrific phone presence, but these same candidates could be extremely disappointing up close and personal. The staff also discovered that it took only a few seconds or minutes to read people, especially candidates who were wrong for the job. So why schedule hours of interviews when less would do? Their solution was the twenty-minute initial interview, which I've called Strategy 10, The Pre-Interview Interview.

Conduct a Brief Pre-Interview Interview

Keep your initial interview short. Although brief meetings are not always practical, they will save more time and energy than you can imagine. Like red and green lights, short interviews are especially helpful with paper tigers who have great resumes but are less impressive in person.

Let's take the example of that not-for-profit organization looking for an office manager. Here's one of their picks in Pile A as determined by the pre-interview letter, resume, and phone call. This candidate's letter began, "I was delighted to learn…" and concluded, "I can easily be reached…" Between these two sentences were specific dates and details. (UCLA, Columbia University, a volunteer in an abused women's clinic. No typos.) In short, she wrote the best letter received. She also interviewed extremely well on the phone. The candidate became one of the ten short interviews scheduled for the following week. However, between the time the candidate parked her car and walked toward the office, she was dead in the water because the assistant director happened to see her drive up in a red Mustang convertible and stride along the sidewalk in the miniskirt to end all miniskirts. She had *attitude* written all over her. Mustang aside, this was true in the waiting room as well. Notwithstanding her fine paper profile and outstanding phone interview, the candidate was wrong for this not-for-profit organization, which worked with inner city adolescents. The cordial twenty-minute meeting strategy saved the staff hours of interview time and an emotional investment in a noncandidate.

Another example is the candidate whose letter wasn't the best, and who wasn't especially brilliant on the phone. But she was good enough to get an initial interview. Her first in-person impression was terrific, though, and the good chemistry was confirmed over the next twenty minutes. She was a recent graduate of Colorado College, and during summer vacations she had worked at a juvenile detention center in Denver. Her references were outstanding. A longer interview was scheduled, followed by a one-week project with the current office manager, who was leaving for a teaching job.

After the week-long tryout, the candidate was hired. The organization had found the right person and saved days or weeks of wasted time.

Here's a summary of Strategies 9 and 10: ☞

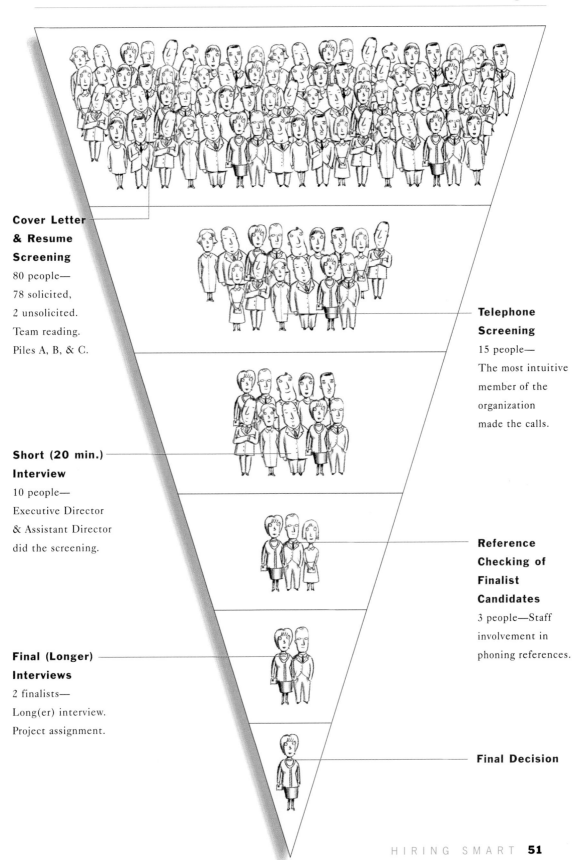

**Cover Letter
& Resume
Screening**
80 people—
78 solicited,
2 unsolicited.
Team reading.
Piles A, B, & C.

**Telephone
Screening**
15 people—
The most intuitive
member of the
organization
made the calls.

**Short (20 min.)
Interview**
10 people—
Executive Director
& Assistant Director
did the screening.

**Reference
Checking of
Finalist
Candidates**
3 people—Staff
involvement in
phoning references.

**Final (Longer)
Interviews**
2 finalists—
Long(er) interview.
Project assignment.

Final Decision

Contents: Chapter 2

Strategies During the Interview

"You can never pay the right person enough, and you always pay the wrong person too much—no matter what the number."

—Charles "Red" Scott,
Vice Chair, Board of Directors,
Pier One Imports, Inc.

Chapter 2: Strategies During the Interview

When planning for an upcoming interview, I've always found it important to remember these three basic assumptions.

1. Interviews test how well someone interviews.

The results may be impressive but misleading. Take the candidate who is attractive, articulate, and skillful in answering interview questions with clear, concise, and even humorous answers. I love such candidates.

Yet where does that leave us? The candidate has just passed the "chemistry" test along with the interview test. We'll probably hire such a candidate if he or she does as well in twenty additional tests.

But interviews can also be misleading. A recent recruiting booklet that serves as a guide for MBA students noted, "Remember, the most qualified candidate does not always get the job. Many times, it's the person who interviews the best who gets the offer."

2. A good con artist can fool you every time.

I have been blindsided in my capacity as a psychiatrist by alcoholic and drug-addicted lawyers and doctors who were so convincing that even *they* didn't know when they were lying. And con artists abound in business. For example, the *Wall Street Journal* ran a front-page story entitled, "Swindler's Tale: How Low-Key Style Let a Con Man Steal Millions from Bosses." "It was just so easy," the mild-mannered bookkeeper said. He could hardly resist.

Once I moderated a panel on "The Biggest Turkey I Ever Picked." "Do you want an embezzler, forger, Don Juan, alcoholic, or run-of-the mill con man?" one of the panelists asked. "I've hired them all. Some, several times!"

3. Interviews in which you induce stress seldom work.

Putting a candidate on the defensive will only demonstrate his or her style of defensive behavior. The strategy may be perfect for predicting winners in football or chess, or when hiring a labor negotiator or defense lawyer, but the reality is that stress puts up walls. The point of an interview, I think, is to take those walls down.

With these three assumptions in mind, here are some tested interviewing tips.

Strategy No. 11:

Trust Your Instincts— Chemistry Is Crucial

Assuming that you've been successful predicting winners in the past, trust your gut. Chemistry is usually determined in the first few minutes of an interview. It's either good, bad, or absent. Where chemistry is important and it's bad or nonexistent, cut the interview short. Prepare all candidates for the initial meeting by saying, in advance, "We'll have a brief initial interview.

Maybe fifteen to twenty minutes, just to meet and say hello."

Harry V. Quadracci started Quad Graphics in 1969 with $250,000 of raised capital, a bank loan, a house mortgage, and a high-tech printing press. Today he is a member of the Forbes 400, and Quad Graphics is a billion-dollar company. He says, "One of our ironclad rules is 'Never do business with anybody you don't like.' If you don't like somebody, there's a reason. Chances are it's because you don't trust them, and you're probably right. I don't care who it is or what guarantees you get— cash in advance, or whatever. If you do business with somebody you don't like, sooner or later you'll get screwed."

Colleen Barrett, the number two executive at Southwest Airlines and the highest ranking woman in the airline industry, put it another way: "Every time I go against my gut, I regret it."

Both these executives are talking about chemistry. When chemistry is good—reflected in smiles, handshakes, eye contact, and enthusiasm—you know it immediately, and you continue with the next series of interview tests.

However, chemistry involves two people. Your feelings are half of the mix. Chemistry is important, but equally important is how you interpret the information you're receiving. For example, I've been told by interviewers: "If I'm tired, I make bad choices." "I hate doing job interviews on Friday afternoons." "I like tall men. If he's six foot five, he has an immediate advantage with me." "If she has a British accent, she sounds smart to me."

Right or wrong, these prejudices exist. In addition, it behooves us to understand which topics are legal and illegal to discuss in an interview. Chemistry is only part of the hiring process, and in a discrimination case, the employer is responsible for articulating credible business reasons for preferring one candidate over the other.

But what if the candidate shows up and we *see* that he's six feet five inches tall? Or seventy-five pounds overweight? Will it make a difference if she speaks with a Brooklyn or a British accent? If he is standing upright or in a wheelchair? If the candidate is an African-American male, or a Hispanic female? In today's diverse world it is absolutely necessary to understand our personal biases so that our initial reactions do not eliminate different, but excellent candidates.

How do we put aside prejudices? If we're conscious about it, we can find what works for us.

Robin Bradford runs a large temporary staffing agency, The Bradford Staff. She knows her prejudices. "If someone is late, it's one of my big biases," she says. "So I've learned to recognize that I'm annoyed and take a deep breath. I also go slower in the interview when I have a prejudice. Actually, some of the best people that I've found over the years are candidates who forced me out of my comfort zone. Otherwise, I'd simply end up hiring people like me."

Bill Gates's bias is a high IQ. He wants brilliant programmers. Consciously or unconsciously, Gates doesn't care about chemistry. Or perhaps he's redefining "chemistry" as our working relationships become more distant in cyberspace.

Nevertheless, when you consider your chemistry with a candidate, be aware of where your feelings are coming from. They may contribute in big ways to the bond or barrier between you and the person you're interviewing.

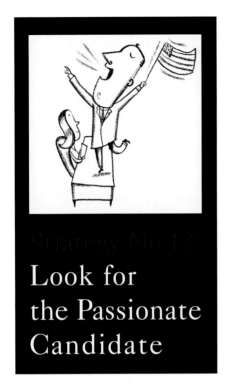

Strategy No. 12:

Look for the Passionate Candidate

Although some lawyers advise that you can't ask directly about the personal passions of the candidate, passion differentiates the exceptional candidates. The passionate candidate will love his job. The passionate candidate is dedicated. The passionate candidate will work hard. When passion is present, the sky is the limit. When passion is missing, all bets are off.

Conventional wisdom tells us that energy and enthusiasm are key ingredients of passionate people, and I agree. But what about unconventional wisdom? Here are three offbeat ideas that you might want to consider.

1. Something to Prove

This may be the essence of passionate people. They're highly motivated. One of the most celebrated examples is Warren Buffett, who wasn't accepted to Harvard Business School. So he went to Columbia, where he met his teacher and future mentor, Benjamin Graham. Buffett has gone on to become the most successful investor in American financial history. Today, when he comes to Harvard Business School, he can't resist mentioning one of his motivations: "I was a Harvard reject."

A less famous case is Paul Orfalea, who was in and out of twelve schools as a young boy. Some teachers thought he was retarded. Later Paul and his family learned that he was severely dyslexic. As a young adult, Paul started a store with one rented copy machine in a 600-square-foot space near Santa Barbara, California. Twenty-five years later, Paul's business, named after the kinky red hair he had as a child, operates 900 stores worldwide. His company is called Kinko's.

2. Athletes, Immigrants, and Entrepreneurs

I like candidates who are passionate about something such as music, sports, computers, books, theater, planes, kids, whatever. A current passion bodes well for future passion on the job. For example, most employers that I know are biased toward athletes, especially amateurs, who have paid their dues. Most athletes who have competed in high school and college understand long hours, teamwork, and discipline.

I also know several executives who are biased toward immigrants, although it is illegal to ask about national origin. They say that their most passionate staff members are first-generation Americans, absolutely dedicated to distinguishing themselves in their new country. Still others look for the passionate candidate among men and women with strong entrepreneurial backgrounds.

Trust your instincts *and* past experience on this one.

3. Hours

Does the person have a track record of working long hours? If so, that's fine. But also beware of those extra hours. Some people try to compensate for a lesser quality of work with a greater quantity of hours. There are also workaholics who can be extraordinarily self-destructive, so long hours can be a double-edged sword. If passion exists beyond the time clock, recognize it, and proceed to the next step.

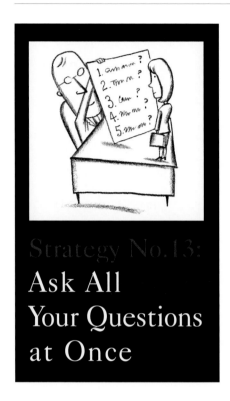

Strategy No.13:

Ask All Your Questions at Once

As the official interview commences, as the starter's gun cracks and the race begins, ask all your questions at once.

That's right. Put all your initial questions on the table up front. This strategy accomplishes three things. First, in a manner of speaking, you pass the baton. You've asked the questions, now the candidate must respond. Performance depends upon the candidate, not selling yourself and the organization.

Second, and more importantly, this strategy directly confronts the most common problem in interviewing: not listening, and talking too much. "I frequently fall in love before the candidate sits down," one friend confessed to me. "Then I start selling before the candidate starts talking." Another businessman said he was aware that "when I talk too much, I telegraph the answers I want."

About 95 percent of the people with whom I work would agree that there's an epidemic of talking too much in interviews. My friend Milo Shelly thinks this is "the most egregious error made by interviewers." He goes on: "I feel many interviewers talk too much, either because they do not know what to ask, or for ego reasons [they need to tell someone how important they are]. In my initial interviews at Gallo, Ernest asked me what were the most important things I did when interviewing. I told him there are three rules, 'Listen, listen, and listen.' He smiled, and we both conducted a very quiet interview trying to out-listen each other."

Third, and this is a corollary to the Gallo story, this technique *forces you to listen.* If there's one practical tip you should try in your next interview, I suggest this one. Asking all your questions at once, and following up later in the interview, allows you to settle back and watch a candidate's behavior as well as listen to his or her words. Adapt a half-dozen questions that fit your style, but ask them all at once.

You might consider such questions as

☞ **What would your former employer say about you—positive and negative?**

☞ **What would your former subordinates say about you?**

☞ **How do you recognize incompetence? What do you do about it?**

☞ **How do you recognize excellence? What do you do with it?**

☞ **What about yourself would you like to improve most?**

☞ **What makes you lose your temper? Tell me about the last time it happened.**

You'll also find over fifty other suggested interview questions on pages 187–190. Even after thirty years as a professional listener, I still need all the help I can get.

Here's an example that illustrates the benefits of this strategy. After a two-day seminar on hiring, a client, George Hume, president and CEO of Basic American, Inc., resolved to make several changes in his hiring process. The first shift was to ask all his questions at once. In his very next interview, about forty-eight hours after our seminar, he showed a prospective chief financial officer candidate around his San Francisco offices. When they arrived back in George's office and the interview officially began, George said, "I just took a seminar on hiring a couple of days ago. Awkward as I feel about doing this, here are the questions that I'd normally ask you over the next hour. Since I tend to talk too much, why don't you just take your time answering and I'll listen." With that, George handed the fellow a sheet of paper with ten questions.

An hour later, as the CFO candidate got ready to leave, he told George that this had been the most exhausting interview in his life. "Why?" George asked, genuinely surprised. "Because," said the fellow, "I've talked for an hour straight, and you've barely said a word." Then he confessed, "I've never talked so much before in my life!"

As George practiced this technique, the interviews became less stressful for him and, consequently, less stressful for his candidates. With the pressure off, George found he became comfortable. He became more animated as he listened, smiling, nodding, even inter-rupting occasionally with such simple prompts as, "Go on... Tell me more... Can you give an example?" That CFO candidate would be far more comfortable answering George's questions today because there's a natural ebb and flow to his interviews. Best of all, asking all his questions at once successfully served George's purpose. It forced him to listen.

I heard the same lesson repeated in a lecture about negotiations. At the end of an expert's talk, an audience member asked the speaker, "What if I pay your hefty fee and spend a day with you? In a sentence, what will I learn watching you in a negotiation?"

"I don't need a sentence. Just two words," the expert negotiator said. "Listen better."

Strategy No.14:

Have Fun During the Interview

Pick two or three "Columbo-type" questions and enjoy yourself. The candidate should respond accordingly, and you'll learn a great deal in the process.

Red Scott's favorite question in an interview is, "Are you lucky?" It's a variation on Henry Ford's favorite question, "Are you curious?" Apocryphal or not, there's a classic story about how Henry Ford always took finalist candidates to lunch. If the finalist salted his food before he tasted it, Ford concluded that the candidate was a creature of habit, and not curious enough to taste a new dish in a strange restaurant. Creatures of habit were not what Henry Ford wanted in his executives.

So why does Red Scott ask, "Are you lucky?" According to Red, if a candidate says, "Yes, I'm lucky—lotteries, raffles, bingo—I always win," it's one less thing for him to worry about. On the other hand, if the candidate says, "No, not really," Red says to himself, "With all my other problems at the company, I certainly don't need this poor guy with his bad luck."

Larry Stupski, the vice chairman of Charles Schwab, a Yale-trained lawyer, and an extraordinarily smart and successful executive, used to play Columbo with his candidates. (Columbo was the seemingly bumbling detective whose disingenuous questions ultimately did in his suspects.) Although Larry knew everything about all the departments that reported to him, including Human Resources, he loved to play a little with Human Resources candidates. "Listen," Larry would say toward the beginning of the interview, "I'm just a legal and financial guy who never really understood the HR department. What exactly does a HR director do?" If the candidate could explain the job in detail, clearly and concisely, Larry went on to the next question. If the candidate spoke in jargon and buzzwords, Larry nodded and smiled, but he always thought, "Gotcha!"

Another successful businessman, Alan Dachs, has fun asking, "How are you going to lose money for me?" It's a curveball, and Alan always listens and watches to see how a candidate answers this legitimate, if surprising, question.

Another CEO, Carl Sewell, who wrote *Customers for Life*, believes that the ultimate hiring test is to see if a candidate fidgets during interviews. He loves energetic folks. Surprisingly, if you can sit still for an interview, you're not his cup of tea.

As a psychiatrist, I like to listen for what a candidate might be leaving out of his story. Like Sherlock Holmes in *The Hound of the Baskervilles,* I listen for the dogs that don't bark. For example, several years ago a friend asked me to interview an engineer who was a candidate to be her chief of operations. All the members of her company's executive board were women, which qualified the company as a minority applicant under affirmative action guidelines for government contracts.

I was asked to meet the candidate, a poised, attractive, forty-five-year-old male West Point graduate, at a West Los Angeles hotel where I was speaking. I had asked him by phone to spend an hour with me. I began the interview by asking all my initial questions at once: "Tell me a little bit about your current job. Then I'd like to hear in more detail about your background, personal and professional, and since we have an hour please take your time. I'll listen, take notes, and probably have a few questions when we finish."

I listened as the ex-army officer discussed at length his career, his father, his brothers, his mentors at West Point, his five-year career in the Corps of Engineers, and his three years with an aerospace outfit in San Diego. In addition, he mentioned two sons. What the ex-captain didn't discuss in his detailed and compelling history were his mother, sisters, wife, and daughters, all presumably alive and well, just missing in action. Missing from a history where the candidate was applying for work in an all-female executive suite.

The candidate's apparent blind spot with women was raised and discussed directly with him, first by me, then by my friend. And because it was identified and predicted in advance, it was open to solution. The candidate was smart enough and motivated enough to succeed and, with that assurance, the executive thought the ex-captain from West Point was the best-qualified candidate for the job. Principled and disciplined, he had compiled a great track record as a successful team player and leader. In addition, my friend wanted a man on her executive committee for diversity, and a man to deal directly with her largely male engineer clientele.

The story ends positively. Despite my initial concerns, the West Point graduate has proved a tremendous asset and great leader for her company.

Strategy No.15:
Assign a Mini-Project to Finalists

Three quarters of the way through the interview, give the candidate a task to perform. Not only does this demonstrate the candidate's behavior—it also breaks the monotony of most interviews.

Here are some specific examples: A large advertising agency in San Francisco shows a potential creative director the rough cut of a new spot for Levi's 501 jeans. The spot features a ninety-two-year-old blues singer in rural Mississippi with two possible soundtracks: one in which the man's raspy voice ends the spot, and one in which his voice is muted over a banjo in the background. What does the candidate think? Obviously there are no right or wrong answers, but the project may bring both practicality and passion into the interview situation. The approach also beats the usual "Why are you interested in our company?" or "Where do you expect to be in five years?"

Crate and Barrel is interviewing for a new marketing position in their corporate offices. By coincidence, the chief buyer for Crate and Barrel has just returned from a shopping trip to Europe with new patio furniture, oversized umbrellas, and pillows. The spring catalog's design and marketing approach for the patio merchandise is in its early stages.

Halfway into the interview, the interviewer asks the candidate how she would market the new furniture and why. Not only does this pull away from standard questions and enliven the interview, it also provides an insight into the candidate's creativity, as well as her practical advice about the new product.

United Electric Controls in Boston implements a competency-based application process for new hires. It includes a lengthy application package and asks for a demonstration of skills. For example, candidates for a machinist position might be asked to interpret a blueprint as part of their pre-interview assignment. Then finalist candidates might be asked to mill or fabricate a part based on that same blueprint.

The assignments make it easier to screen applicants. For one thing, only 50 percent of prospective hires complete and return the application! According to United Electric Controls, candidates who are selected for interviews express appreciation at having the opportunity to demonstrate their skills.

A design firm is doing an annual report for Time Warner at the same time a serious design candidate is being interviewed by several partners in their New York offices. In a bar graph showing Warner Brothers' revenues, the design staff has incorporated the Bugs Bunny logo. The interviewer asks the candidate, "What do you think? Does the cartoon work? What visuals might work better?"

Lexicon Branding Inc. charges Fortune 500 companies as much as $40,000 to come up with the right name for a product. Recently, Lexicon began running regional ads in publications such as *Adweek*, inviting West Coast wordsmiths to test their creativity. Under the headline "Natural Born Namers," the copy invites applicants to submit ten names for a network operating system and another ten for either a mountain bike or a new citrus-flavored soft drink. Applicants who show promise are given additional assignments.

Let's say that an ad agency's creative candidate has a reel of his ten years in advertising, condensed down to fifteen minutes. Is it worth seeing? Absolutely. It will tell you more about his creative abilities than a mini-project. And Crate and Barrel's marketing candidate, presumably, has a lengthy portfolio of her own work produced over her ten or twenty years in the business. All aspects of these mini-projects—those you initiate, and those that the candidate volunteers—count before and after the interview toward the twenty or 200 plays you need to observe before you pick the right candidate for you.

Strategy No. 16:

Seek Closure by Announcing the Five-Minute Warning

"We have about five more minutes..." is a useful statement before closure. Pay attention to "By the way...," "Oh, one more thing...," and "I almost forgot...," which mean, "This is the most important thing I'm going to say."

Announcing that there's five minutes left in an interview is like telling a marathon runner that you're at mile 26 and the finish line is in sight. With the end in sight, performance changes.

In my psychiatry practice, I always announced that we were coming to the end of an hour, both as the timekeeper, and because I knew there was another patient in my waiting room. The announcement served as a flashing yellow light. Slow down or speed up—we're about to stop. I also learned that men and women invariably say something that's really important at this point, regardless of the time you've already spent together.

For this particular insight I can thank a patient who drove 150 miles from Lake Tahoe to see me every Friday. With five minutes left in one session, he announced, "Oh, by the way, I keep forgetting..." Then the man told me he had a mistress in San Francisco with whom he spent Friday nights. "Since my wife is all in favor of my late Friday afternoon appointments with you," he explained, "I can get away with spending the night in San Francisco. Therapy is the perfect cover."

And I had thought the man was driving 150 miles because I was such a great therapist!

Later, I began consulting to businesspeople who also had experiences with last-minute revelations. They'd be taken to lunch by a client and not until dessert or coffee would the client cough and announce, "By the way...," which was always the prelude to the *real* reason for the meeting.

If you've had a good interview and the candidate feels relatively comfortable, you may expect a variety of surprises after you've indicated that the interview is almost over, and not just around the job description and compensation, but about more personal issues. For instance, a candidate for a plant manager's job said to me, with five minutes to go in our interview, "Let me ask you, is Andrea serious? Do we really have to work on Saturday mornings? I've always coached Little League on Saturday morning. If I couldn't coach on weekends, my wife and kids would kill me."

I didn't know the answer, but I thought it was better to find out today about the Saturday morning expectation than to be surprised and disappointed tomorrow. The candidate asked me to discuss it with Andrea because he knew that I had a relationship with her. And Andrea told me, "He misunderstood. If work isn't done by the weekend, we work on Saturday mornings. However, I don't care if he works late Wednesday or Thursday nights. Just so his work is finished by Friday night." Subsequently, Andrea and the candidate discussed Saturdays directly, and the plant manager took the new job with one less hidden agenda.

Another personal experience that I've had with last-minute issues involved a sales manager who had been recruited while he was working for another firm. With five minutes to go in our interview, the man said, "I should tell you that I really can't consider the new job."

"Why?" I asked. "Because I'm worried about health insurance coverage." And with this, the candidate teared up. "I have a five-year-old daughter who has been diagnosed with leukemia," he told me. His health insurance covered his little girl for doctors, hospitals, chemotherapy, and radiation, but the illness had been a nightmare. "And if we cancel our health insurance because I change jobs, it's going to be an even bigger nightmare, which we can't afford." Then he asked, "What do you suggest?"

There was no alternative. We put the issue on the table, talked with lawyers and insurance brokers, consulted the company's benefits person, and learned that the company had a policy in which no pre-existing condition for a new employee's family could be excluded. But if this health issue hadn't surfaced at the end of the interview process, this excellent candidate would never have shifted jobs while still attempting to protect his family.

Strategy No. 17.

Watch for Inappropriate Behavior

Pay attention to a candidate's behavior, not words, especially if you can't explain the candidate's behavior during the selection process. Consider alcohol and drugs whenever you see inappropriate behavior in an otherwise qualified candidate.

Not long ago I was visiting a college campus in New York with two guests who were potential donors to the school. Coincidentally, the college president had asked me to interview one of his department chairs for a dean's position at the Albany campus. We arranged for a half-hour's visit after lunch with the department chair, who would also answer questions from my guests. Later, I would arrange a formal interview without the visitors.

Then a funny thing happened. Although he knew my guests had just toured the campus for two hours, and by their own admission had tons of questions about the college, the candidate couldn't stop talking. And not only talking, but talking like a machine gun. Without pausing to inhale—let alone listen—the man spoke in a stream of consciousness about his own history, achievements, honors, and awards in an unparalleled display of insecurity that I've never witnessed before or since.

I discussed the episode with the college president and selection committee in a conference call. "Robert's" antennae were clearly broken that day. What did his behavior mean? Was it anxiety, insecurity, or a personal problem? The president felt that Robert should be included in our discussion, and I agreed, since the deanship was too critical a job to ignore such egregious behavior. Although I would have preferred to discuss the incident face to face, Robert was asked to join the committee in the conference call, during which I again summarized my observations.

Surprisingly, Robert agreed. "Yes, that's exactly what happened," he began. (Would I have been so candid? I doubt it. My first instinct would have been defensive, especially if I wanted the deanship as much as I knew Robert wanted it.) But he said, "You're right," and he continued without missing a beat. "It must be the pressure. If we move to Albany, I'd have to sell the house in Scarsdale and pull our daughter out of high school where she's finally made some close friends. My wife's also against the move, so the tension at our house is rather palpable these days. Obviously the stress must be affecting me more than I'd care to admit."

With this candor, Robert had effectively defused the situation. The potential adversarial relationship with the president and selection committee had become a cooperative one. The crucial question was how to solve the family situation, and after Robert left the conference call, the selection committee began to discuss it.

I remained skeptical about his candidacy. Robert's behavior still seemed grossly inappropriate. Yet despite my contrary position, the selection committee voted that afternoon to offer Robert the job, and he took it.

Of course, I make mistakes every day. But I wouldn't be telling this story unless there was an "X factor"—an unknown wild card issue—in Robert's case. Two years after he was hired, Robert was fired from the deanship in Albany. Robert was an alcoholic who had hidden his problem from the college for years. He had also survived in a dysfunctional family system that included a codependent wife and a daughter who had escaped by living much of the time with her friends.

With this piece of the puzzle in place, the picture became clearer. Alcohol, as well as stress, probably played a role in the candidate's compulsive talking that day. Our visit with the potential donors had been hastily arranged and occurred after lunch. Robert may have had an elevated blood alcohol level that I had never considered as an "X factor" during our time together.

Strategy No.18:

Identify Strengths & Weaknesses

No one is good at everything. We play to our strengths. But the reality is that our strengths, in the extreme, may predict our weaknesses. Therefore ask candidates about their strengths, and consider what might exist on the other side of the looking glass.

Recently, on behalf of a client, I interviewed an excellent candidate. The chemistry was immediate, clear, and mutual. The candidate had an impressive background, spoke well, used specific examples, and displayed a marvelous sense of humor. Consequently, I asked the company's president to schedule a second meeting with him.

En route to his meeting the candidate called to say, "Thank you for your vote of confidence. I know the president wouldn't meet with me again without your recommendation. I won't let you down. Thanks again."

Suffice it to say that such a phone call is unique, confirming not only chemistry, but also the young man's people skills and motivation to succeed. I was impressed.

But what is the downside of such chemistry, charisma, and charm? Several days later, the results from the candidate's psychological test, interpreted by an expert in Atlanta, arrived at my office.

Outstanding Characteristics:

This is an extremely sociable, persuasive, and garrulous individual who will keep pushing forward to win his objectives with a tremendous amount of self-confidence. Although possessing goodwill towards others, he is very much interested in making a good impression, both personally and for the company.

Possible Limitations Under Pressure:

Because he has a strong need for acceptance, he may have a tendency to be more concerned with popularity than with results, telling others what they want to hear. He may have a tendency to oversell…

This candidate's strengths in the extreme were weaknesses that needed to be anticipated in the new job. The strength of this "nice guy" was his spirit of cooperation. But did he avoid conflict and confrontation? Another strength was his leadership, but did he suffer from a thin skin and take criticism personally? A final strength was his desire for harmony. Yet a common weakness in such candidates is that they sweep problems under the rug.

Identifying strengths and weaknesses doesn't exactly predict the future, but it identifies possibilities you'll want to consider as you watch a candidate for any high-level position. In this case the employer decided against the candidate, of whom he was very distrustful.

The interesting phenomenon of strengths that can also be weaknesses is demonstrated by the results of an airline's test conducted in a North American training facility that attracts pilots from all over the world. Ninety-seven percent of the three-day testing program on sophisticated flight simulators involves "by the book" expertise. Pilots perform routine and emergency flight safety procedures as prescribed by FAA regulations and standard flight manuals. In worldwide competition, I'm told that pilots from Pan Pacific Airlines (a pseudonym) achieve the highest scores ninety-seven percent of the time.

The question is: If their strengths are obvious, what are their weaknesses? Three percent of the annual flight test assesses flexibility, innovation, and creative solutions to problems not covered by FAA regulations or flight manuals. When it comes to "flying by the seat of one's pants," Pan Pacific pilots can't compete. Their strict adherence to rules and regulations has its limitations. When they get away from standard operating procedures, all bets are off.

A United pilot, Sandy Beebe, told me a more detailed story that "wasn't guaranteed to be completely factual," but his point is good.

One Pan Pacific regulation states that evacuations must be initiated by the cockpit crew. So when a Pan Pacific airplane hit a barrier just a little short of a runway and caught fire, it was a problem. Why?

Because the crew remained silent. As the cabin filled with smoke, a United flight attendant who happened to be a passenger on board finally yelled, "Hey, we're on fire! We have to evacuate," and he started opening exits. With no crew in sight, he ran into the cockpit and flung open the door. Incredibly, the cockpit crew was just sitting there. Again, the United steward said, "The plane's burning up. You have to get off," but the crew didn't budge. Finally, the Pan Pacific pilot said something about having lost honor, and that he and his crew would stay with the plane.

The Pan Pacific cockpit crew never did give the order to evacuate and died in the accident. Yet all the passengers managed to get out in time thanks to the United flight attendant's training and actions in the emergency.

The reality is that United flight attendants are given the training and authority to act on their own. When a plane stops, they can initiate an evacuation if they see smoke or flames.

This happened in the famous "Iowa cornfield crash" of United Flight 232, when the plane's No. 2 engine exploded in a hail of shrapnel, and the flight controls were destroyed. As the plane meandered through the Iowa skies, climbing and descending, Captain Al Haynes and his crew fought a futile battle with, unbeknownst to them, unpowered controls. However, a United training instructor named Dennis Fitch, who was a passenger on board, sensed that problems existed and volunteered to help. "Send him up. We can use all the help we can get," said Captain Haynes. Only in retrospect did the crew learn that Fitch alone, kneeling on the cockpit floor and making power changes to keep the plane upright, controlled the plane.

When United 232 crash-landed in the Iowa cornfield, the cockpit broke off. All three pilots, plus that volunteer on his knees manipulating the plane's thrust without a seat belt, were thrown several hundred feet away. They couldn't give any evacuation commands. So once again it was the United flight attendants who ultimately gave the order for an emergency evacuation.

Pilot Haynes, together with Fitch and all but one of his flight crew, were among the survivors. When Iowa's governor visited Al Haynes in the hospital, he found the pilot distraught. "I lost that baby," Haynes told the governor, crying. "I understand Captain Haynes is very upset," said Sister Mary Viannea, a seventy-seven-year-old nun who had been carried to safety by other passengers. "He shouldn't be. He did the best he could, and his directions were splendid."

My friend Sandy Beebe concludes, "Al Haynes is a true hero. Talk about strengths and flexibility: Captain Haynes used *all* resources available to him, and in the process, he saved 186 passengers."

Strategy No. 19:

Pick a Subject Where You Are the Expert

The rule of thumb is: If candidates can go into detail and depth about a subject, they probably have some expertise in that area. If not, the opposite is true. On the other hand, the key is to ask questions in *your areas of expertise.*

Since I know very little about finance or marketing, I rarely ask questions about these specialties, except "Give me a five-minute summary." However, I do ask a rather simple question, such as "Tell me about an employee you had to fire." Although it's only one piece of a 200-piece puzzle, one middle-aged candidate gave an answer that I'd never heard before: "Sorry. I've never fired anyone." Of course, we continued the interview without missing a beat.

Compare that answer with another candidate's response: "I thought about it for weeks, waking up at night, going over what I'd say. My stomach was in knots, yet I knew the person's performance was mediocre and reasons for his termination were well-documented. However, the time was never right since I was always out of town on Fridays, the best day to terminate an employee. No, that's a rationalization. The truth is that I hate firing people, and this was no exception.

"So I called an outplacement firm and got their advice, plus an outplacement executive to come to our offices on that fateful Friday. The meeting was straightforward. We went through various financial packages that gave the employee some control over the process. Of course he felt out of control. What about his performance reviews, future, reputation, wife, children, and everything else? Despite an at-will clause in his employment agreement that protected the company, the more the man said in my office, I knew the less likely he'd be to consult an attorney. Anyway, we shook hands, and he went down the hall to meet with the outplacement executive. Fortunately, the fellow found a great job within three months. But I still get upset thinking about that situation."

Another candidate said about a similar circumstance: "The guy wasn't performing. That's the bottom line. So I fired him. If you want more details, I'd be happy to go into them."

Do you prefer a thoughtful and complete answer, or a no-nonsense approach to your question? It's your call, and whatever suits your style is the right answer. In this case, I thought both candidates knew what they were talking about. On the other hand, when an experienced individual says he's never fired an employee in his life, and no details are forthcoming, whistles and bells should go off.

Strategy No.20:

Take Notes During the Interview

Use a pad with a line drawn down the middle. On one side of the page, make appropriate notes about what the candidate tells you regarding jobs, dates, strengths, weaknesses, etc. On the other side, note what you're thinking. Nothing is too minor to write down: questions, missing pieces, thoughts, feelings, likes, dislikes. Both sides of your pad will be very influential as you make your decision.

Here's an example of notes from an interview with a candidate for vice president of finance with a start-up software company. On the right are the initial notes of what I heard during the interview; on the left are the abridged notes of my reactions to the candidate.

What I am thinking:	What the candidate is saying:
1st... 1st... 1st...	MBA to Morgan Stanley
Why is he so driven?	Father was a CPA
Where does he let down?	Mother was a bookkeeper.
Smart guy	660 Math, 640 English on SAT
Verbal guy	US Army—3 years
Can he go to a bottom-up organization?	Arthur Andersen—2 years
Can he give up control?	Peat Marwick—3 years

(Note: If a legal question arises about a person's employment, your notes can always be requested. So keep in mind the guidelines on pages 202–208.)

Strategy No.21:
Interview in Teams for Top Candidates

Interviewing in teams is a rare, but thorough means of evaluating candidates. Although it's very hard to coordinate interview schedules, it's often worth the effort and is an example of hiring smart instead of managing tough.

Four executives met with me to discuss how to streamline their hiring procedures. The group included a corporate counsel with a legal background, a human resources director who had worked with Coopers & Lybrand, a recruiting director with a degree in business from Notre Dame, and a newly hired manager who had recently left a successful chain of grocery stores in Arizona. Joining us at the last minute was a fifth executive, an ex–basketball player from Stanford University who brought with him a prospective candidate. The candidate had agreed to be our guinea pig. We would use a team interview with him as a way to begin our reevaluation of their selection process.

Despite our opening disclaimer—"This must be stressful"—the candidate seemed unusually relaxed. The interview went well, and after the meeting the ex–basketball player and his candidate departed for San Francisco while we discussed the man's performance.

Since the candidate faced an obviously intimidating group of potential employers, the lawyer felt that the candidate's performance was remarkable. "He was so relaxed," the attorney observed. The accountant-turned-human-resources-director also couldn't believe the candidate's comfort level. "Under the same circumstances," she said, "I would have dissolved completely." The recruiting director was impressed by the candidate's MBA-style discussion about "exit strategies" and "shareholder value."

The grocery store alumnus who'd been with the new company for two weeks spoke last. "The candidate loved performing for us," she began. "Frankly, I distrust all that MBA mumbojumbo about exit strategies and shareholder value when the real question is 'How is he going to manage people?' Besides, I thought he was arrogant as hell. Can you imagine a blue-collar customer in a grocery store coming up to this yuppie snob with a question about toothpaste or dish soap? Can he talk to working people? I don't think so. So do we really want him as one of our managers?"

"But how do you really feel?" the lawyer asked.

We all laughed but ultimately came to agree with the manager's insights. Here we had all the "usual suspects" in the team interview—a lawyer, an accountant, a business major, an athlete, and a psychiatrist. But it was the new kid on the block, talking about toothpaste and dish soap, who emerged as the group's best reader of people.

Strategy No.22:

Ask for a Legal Release

Employment discrimination cases are surging into the federal courts in record numbers, more than doubling in the past four years. New laws. New attitudes. So have the candidate sign whatever releases are relevant. In our litigious society, this play is, unfortunately, as basic as breathing in and breathing out. On pages 196–201 you'll find generic releases for California candidates that your counsel can adapt accordingly.

Let me simplify a complicated question: When is it important for a candidate to sign a legal release? Many small employers don't use them at all, but Robin Bradford, who hires 4,000 temporary employees a year, says, "People do hide things and make misrepresentations. I have all candidates sign a release form, an at-will clause, and an arbitration agreement three times during the hiring process. They sign when they fill out an application, co-sign an employment agreement, and after they read our policy and procedures manual. Additionally, if they misrepresent themselves, it's grounds for termination. I also send out a cover letter that says, in effect, 'We're very happy to offer you a position,' and I go on to say, 'I apologize for the formality of this letter, but I am sure you will agree that it is important for us to document all employment relationships carefully.' A four-page letter and legal document follow."

This is a complicated subject, and employment law has become a growth industry. Discuss it with your attorney. It's your call.

Strategy No. 23:

Throw a Few Curveballs at the End of the Interview

Do something unpredictable after the interview, like walking the candidate to his car. Note make, model, location, and anything else that says something personal about the candidate. Look for surprises.

After the official interview ends, I like to walk candidates to their cars. Cars tell a lot about a person. Once I met a rather odd candidate who arrived late to our interview. He was a prospect for the sales manager's job at a chain of retail stores. Afterward, we walked to the man's car, which was parked at an angle to the curb and stuffed with clutter, clothes, tools, and newspapers piled up to the windows. As dogs sometimes look like their owners, so did this man's car look like him.

Several weeks later a developer showed up for our interview in a tailored pinstripe suit, Gucci shoes, Ferragamo tie, and gold ring. Ironically, I happened to know the man was down on his luck and had been for the past three years. Yet he still drove a $100,000 Mercedes, which announced that appearances remained very important to him. My task was therefore to get beyond those appearances.

I know one fellow who asks potential salesmen to drive him on the freeway to the post office or shopping center, not only to see the candidate's car, but also to ascertain how aggressive, assertive, and risk-taking the salesman is. Whereas the sales candidate knows enough to sound assertive in an interview, he may paradoxically drive in the slow lane. Although I've never driven with a salesman, nor equated driving styles with salesmanship, this man swears by his driving test.

There are other examples. Investor extraordinaire Warren Buffett supposedly drives an old car. He thinks cars speak volumes about a person's values. And one of San Francisco's finest criminal defense lawyers drives a $100 Rent-a-Wreck because he believes in recycling. Even in cases where the car doesn't reveal anything significant, a person's behavior outside of the office, with the comfort of his car nearby, may tell you something.

An executive who had just interviewed a candidate gave me a call. "This guy is great," the regional manager began. "See what you think next Thursday. After you see him, I'd like to make a job offer."

The candidate was a mid-thirties, fit, attractive male who had recently worked for a Wall Street firm in their investment banking department. His personal history was straightforward. He had a close family, his parents were lawyers, and his siblings had attended Eastern prep schools and then Duke, Virginia, and Tulane. In addition, the candidate was a leader and athlete, having played quarterback on the varsity football team in college, run marathons, and served as president of his fraternity.

His presentation was pretty much perfect, so I asked, "Where are you less than perfect? How do you let down? Where do you get angry? As a former football player and marathon runner, where does your natural competitiveness come out?"

It wasn't that the candidate didn't understand the questions. He did, but he couldn't answer. He shrugged and said, "My fiancée asks me the same questions."

I tried again later in the interview and got nowhere. By the time the candidate was prepared to leave my office, I still felt that a major piece of the puzzle was missing, and I offered to walk him to his car to go over his return route to the airport. Standing on the sidewalk, with the interview officially over, I asked another question the candidate hadn't answered earlier: "Why are you really leaving your job?" But this time I added something personal, like "Working on Wall Street must have a downside. My son is in business school and isn't terribly impressed with most of the investment bankers he meets."

Bingo.

About to get into his car, the ex-college quarterback let loose with a stream of expletives concerning his life and bosses on Wall Street and how they were all trying to "screw" him by firing him a day before his bonus was due. Half kidding, I said, "I hope you have a good lawyer." And boy did he!

Welcome to the nineties.

At least we had an answer to the questions "Where do you get angry? How does your competitiveness come out? And why are you leaving the company now?" Yet those missing pieces of the puzzle only became clear well after the official interview ended, and I had walked the candidate to his car where we held our curbside chat.

My biggest surprise walking a candidate to his car was when I discovered the candidate's wife sitting inside the automobile, waiting for him. She and her husband knew our interview was to last two hours. Why wasn't she in my waiting room? Why didn't the candidate suggest a soft drink from my kitchen? Why didn't she walk five minutes into the town of Mill Valley? Two hours in a hot car on a warm August day said more about the candidate and his relationship with his wife, and her acceptance of that relationship, than any of my questions in the interview.

Against my recommendation, the man was hired for an operation in Arizona. Predictably, his relationship with female employees was an unmitigated disaster. Threatened with litigation, he lasted less than a year. However, my client had wanted "the next warm body that walked into the office," and he got that warm body. It calls to mind the familiar curse "Be careful of what you wish for—it may come true." Or as Saint Thérèse said, "More tears are shed over answered prayers than unanswered ones."

Contents: Chapter 3

Strategies After the Interview

"Quality individuals are always great hires. Those that lack quality are always bad hires. No exceptions ever to this rule."

—Jim Bunch, Partner,
Green, Manning & Bunch,
Denver, Colorado

Chapter 3: Strategies After the Interview

I'm a fly fisherman. Although I've never mastered the art of fly fishing, the idea is relatively simple: Find where the trout are feeding. Match the fly hatch. Cast across the river with your line so your fly and line float naturally downstream. Pray that at least one trout is hungry enough to take your bait. Feel the nibble. Pause. Set the hook. Pull back with authority. And catch the big one, right?

Wrong, because in fly fishing that's only half the story, and the next steps are equally crucial: Hold a strong, upright rod and keep a taut line. Allow the trout to run downstream. Reel the fish upstream, then allow the trout to swim downstream in an ebb and flow, an instinctual dance of life and survival, which ends with your catching and, I hope, releasing that magnificent trout back into the river to fight another day. The point is that just when you think the game is over, you find half the battle ahead of you.

The same is true with hiring excellent people. Half the battle remains after the candidate leaves your office. If you cease observing behavior after you've completed the interview, it's like hooking the fish but neglecting to catch him. If you keep your eyes and ears open during this crucial post-interview phase of the selection process, you'll learn more about the candidate's behavior and track record than you ever thought possible.

Strategy No. 24:

Ask for a Return Call from the Candidate

This strategy is designed to save time, and I always use it. Before a candidate leaves my office I make a simple request. "Please call me back on Monday." It's a quick, easy way to observe behavior and another chance to pass that 800-pound hiring gorilla over to the candidate.

I say, "You'll probably have a few thoughts on the way home, maybe some questions, so let's talk for five minutes, even to touch base, if you're available by phone next week." Then we settle on a time and day. Surprisingly, 15 percent of finalist candidates miss the call. Hard to believe? I thought so, too, but the following note from Oklahoma is typical of many I have received over the years.

Dear Pierre,

Today, while negotiating with an unknown out-of-town contractor, I asked him to call me back between 1:00 and 2:00 p.m. with answers to certain questions. His failure to do so set off alarm systems and helps to confirm some suspicions that he may not be disciplined enough to perform in a timely way on a very "time critical" project.

Thanks again for your efforts.

Assign a Take-Home Project

Give finalist candidates a current project you're evaluating and ask for an analysis.

I have suggested that you assign a mini-project in Strategy 15 as part of your technique during the interview. In addition, I suggest that you always give finalist candidates a post-interview project that evaluates attention to detail, as well as the ability to analyze problems and suggest solutions. Here are some examples.

Tony Garnier runs a publicly held water company in Southern California. Looking at a possible acquisition, Tony says to a CFO finalist, "We're thinking of an acquisition in New Mexico. Here's some nonconfidential financial data." (He hands over stacks and stacks of paper.) "How would you advise me?" Then Tony waits to see how timely the candidate's response is and how good his analysis is.

Robin Bacci runs a privately held, $80 million family business in Northern California. She asks a finalist candidate to return for a second visit and discusses the wisdom of adding a Lexus franchise to her Mercedes dealership. Together she and the potential general manager drive around the neighborhood discussing possible sites for a new franchise. Then Robin asks the candidate to prepare a brief proposal regarding site selection should she get the franchise.

Kirsty Melville of Ten Speed Press, a book publisher in the San Francisco Bay Area, is looking for a top-notch copy editor who is fast and accurate. Candidates who impress the managing editor are given an unedited chapter to take home. They then mail the finished work back. In this same firm, applicants for editorial assistantships are asked to evaluate one of the slew of book proposals that are always on hand. The applicant then returns the proposal with a written review and recommendation.

Aside from the quality of work, you'll learn a bit more about the candidate; how long it takes them to return the material, for instance. Does the candidate bother to send it back by priority mail? What shape is the material in when it comes back—are there coffee rings on the pages?

Take-home projects allow candidates to show you their best work. Then you're able to judge if their best is good enough.

Strategy No. 26:

Travel with Finalists for Executive Positions

If one picture is worth a thousand words, then one trip is worth a hundred interviews.

Rather than evaluate information he might collect in the course of more interviews, the founder of a growing restaurant chain set up a series of post-interview tests with a finalist for a vice president position. One was a trip.

He met the candidate at the San Diego airport for a 7:00 A.M. flight. The founder was there at 6:15, and the potential VP—also a morning person, as he later explained—arrived at 6:20. With extra time, these executives were able to talk and upgrade their seats on the plane. Later, between planes in Salt Lake, the founder watched the candidate deal with a crisis by phone.

To him the candidate appeared focused in the telephone conversation, and as far as the man could tell, helpful in the situation. When they arrived in Montana an hour later, their destination was an airport hotel some 300 yards from where they stood waiting for an airport shuttle bus. The candidate suggested they walk and carry the bags the several hundred yards to their hotel, which was, literally, three minutes by foot from the airport. Clearly the candidate's travel behavior was as important as his interviews in the company's offices because the pattern continued as the two men traveled from city to city. On time. Good spirits. Problem solver. Great presence with employees and customers. After a two-year search involving a half dozen finalists and several search firms, the candidate was declared the winner by the end of the trip.

Then a funny thing happened. The job negotiations took a strange twist. The candidate became not only tough, but stubborn, and not only stubborn, but he crossed the line from hard bargaining to self-destructiveness. Travel aside, his subsequent behavior threatened to blow the negotiations, as well as his future job, out of the water. The founder's hunch was that the candidate was in the process of destroying whatever trust and goodwill he had built during the months of interviews and several days of travel, and so he told the candidate. But he was wrong.

As the executive's behavior during the trip indicated, he was to become a truly outstanding executive. In retrospect, his negotiating behavior only foreshadowed his negotiating toughness—nothing more, nothing less—a toughness that proved to be an enormous asset to the restaurant chain. With the new VP's strong hand, the company bought and built in locations across America in advance of a successful initial public offering.

The lesson here is to be prepared for twists and unexpected turns. Don't count someone out of the running based on one or two plays.

Strategy No.27:

Meet the Spouse or Significant Other

It's illegal to ask about a candidate's marital status, but the practice is widespread, especially with candidates for top executive positions. If the opportunity arises during the selection process, you may learn a great deal if you meet the candidate's spouse or significant other, if they have one. One's partner is, after all, a hidden player, a key person without whose support even great hires are doomed to failure.

A partner speaks volumes about a candidate. How does the candidate treat their spouse? And vice versa? What worries or anxieties does that person have about the candidate's possible job? What about their own job? If a relocation is involved, what about new housing, neighborhood, schools, doctors, friends, family, temple, or church? Frankly, I can't imagine not addressing these complex concerns. Nevertheless, a majority of employers only superficially ask about family interests, preferring instead to explore a candidate's financial interests. Whereas both are critical, the following story illustrates how important family and friends are to a candidate's spouse.

Some time ago I chaired a panel discussion titled "Crises in My Life." One of the more affecting speakers was the wife of a contractor who had moved to Northern California with their young family nearly twenty years earlier. She had known no one in California, but she had kept house and raised her small children, and she described in some detail her ensuing loneliness over the first six months. "I was so desperate to talk with another adult," she said. "I'd make a trip to the supermarket and deliberately bump into people with my shopping cart just to hear the sound of another adult voice!"

For the candidate worried about his sick child's health insurance, or about missing Little League practice with his son, or about his spouse's isolation, these issues need to be addressed, fully and satisfactorily, *in advance* of new employment. If a wife or husband opposes a new job, and these concerns aren't dealt with in the hiring process, I can almost guarantee that the job will be short-lived.

Strategy No. 28:
Put Potential Problems on the Table

If you're still interested in the candidate, always have a final interview in which you talk about potential problems. It's never a question of *if* problems will arise on a new job, but *what* those problems will be. If you've not discovered any, you're missing something in the candidate's background.

Several years ago, I evaluated an executive who was a finalist candidate for a local company. On a scale of one to ten, I thought the woman was a ten. But in the course of our time together, two potential problems surfaced. First, her husband was unemployed. How would he feel if she was making an executive salary and he remained out of work? Second, how long would the candidate's future mentor at the new company, the chief operating officer, remain in his post? Understandably, the candidate didn't want to begin a new job only to have a key reason for her interest in the company, her potential mentor, leave two months after she accepted the position.

In both cases, I asked the candidate to discuss the matters with her husband, and with the chief operating officer. Her follow-up was predictable and unpredictable. Predictable, because the candidate raised the question directly with her future boss who said, "Eighty percent I'll stay on." Willing to take the 80/20 odds, the candidate assumed the COO would keep her posted if she accepted the job. Unpredictable, because the candidate discussed her husband's sense of self-esteem in a disarmingly candid way. She said, in essence:

"I didn't tell you this during our first meeting, but my husband and I have been trying to have children for several years. I'm forty-two years old and we've had all the tests; I've even taken fertility drugs, but no luck. So we've given up on a larger family, even though we'd love to have children. However, for the past few months we've been reevaluating our marriage and our lives. Do I work? Does he work? Do we adopt children? What's our next step after a very difficult five years? And that's where our discussions led after you interviewed me last week. My husband knows that I want the job, and he thinks it's worth a try regardless of his job prospects. Should we choose to adopt children, it will take six months to a year. Meanwhile, my husband will continue to look for work, and we'll see what the future holds."

To say that I was impressed would be an understatement. How rare it is to see such candor, humanity, and intelligence operating in an interview situation with a relative stranger. Although the candidate was later hired by the company, I was wrong about her being a ten. She was a twelve!

Count on discovering problems with candidates. Your goal is to address whatever difficulties might arise. Here is another example.

After a two-year search, a college president found the perfect academic dean. She was comfortable with herself (a rarer quality than you might expect), and she was highly respected in her profession. Soft-spoken, intelligent, with a proven track record, the new dean discussed stress after we'd spent several hours together.

She suffered from severe migraine headaches. As one with an intermittent history of migraines, I'm particularly sympathetic when a person dons sunglasses because of bright light and admits she's recovering from a migraine attack.

The reality is that we all have ways of dealing with stress. In fact, I almost always ask candidates, "How do you release tension?" The answers vary from "meditation" to "I yell at the dog."

If we can talk openly about absorbing stress, as I do with most of the perfectionistic people I know, then we can also talk about solutions. In the case of the college dean, exercise was the answer. As a perk in the contract we negotiated, we included a gym membership at a fitness center near the college campus. The woman could easily take time in the mornings or afternoons or early evenings, depending on her own preference, to spend time working out. Assuming the deanship would be stressful, the goal was not only to predict problems, which are inevitable, but also to incorporate solutions that have been helpful in the past. The gym membership seemed like an inexpensive solution in the dean's case, and it was.

Strategy No.29:

Use an Intuitive Person in the Selection Process

Use a person with the gift of intuition to help in the evaluation of candidates. This may be a spouse, a board member, a consultant, a receptionist, or a friend.

One expert I knew was a former patient of mine. From the age of five to nearly ten, during World War II, she had hidden from the Nazis in a Dutch closet in a second-floor apartment, a flight of stairs the only access to her hiding place. The girl's ability to hear a key turn in a lock, muted conversation, footsteps in a hallway—or most importantly, up the stairway—honed her senses and taught her about people. Her survival had depended upon her senses. Was the person on the stairs a friend or a stranger? German or Dutch? Was it her stepfather? Was he drunk or sober? Happy or sad? Exhausted or rested? She could tell by the footsteps whether to stay hidden or come out of the closet. As an adult, that woman could tell you more about a person's behavior than anyone I have ever met. Although I've never asked this woman to interview a candidate, nor asked a candidate to walk up a flight of stairs for her, the reality is that experts come from a variety of strange and common backgrounds.

Here are several examples of experts that we encounter every day. The car salesman, for instance, sees what you drive in with and can make certain predictions based on that. The shoe clerk knows your story by glancing at your shoes. The clothing salesperson, like a casting agent, sizes up your character at twenty yards. A good newspaper reporter smells the real story and evaluates the storyteller before the interview starts.

A client of mine tells the story of having spent four hours interviewing a finalist for a financial position. Afterward his secretary asked, "What did you think of that fellow?"

"He's okay," the executive replied.

"I rode up in the elevator with him this morning," the secretary said. "He had a bad haircut, and he was wrong for the job."

"She knew it in the elevator!" her boss told me. He realized that his intuitive secretary could have saved him four hours of intensive interviews that ended with the same conclusion.

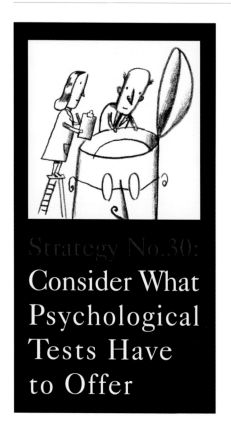

Strategy No. 30:
Consider What Psychological Tests Have to Offer

I like to give prospective employees a fifteen-minute psychological inventory, which I ask them to return by regular mail or fax the next morning. I'm a believer in the value of psychological testing as part of the hiring process, particularly if the test results converge on a potential problem. I also believe that the skill of your evaluator is far more important than the kind of test you use. Does the expert have a proven track record? Can she accurately predict behavior based upon a short pen-and-paper test? If so, testing is extremely useful. (See pages 210–213 for several tests and experts I use.) One caveat: Some courts in some states have concerns about psychological testing. If such tests are used to disclose a mental disability, for example, they could be grounds for a discrimination claim under the Americans with Disabilities Act. So always consult an attorney if you have questions about whether you can ask a candidate to take a particular test.

I've used the Myers-Briggs Type Inventory (MBTI) for almost twenty years because of its simplicity and predictive reliability. I ask a candidate, "Have you ever taken the Myers-Briggs? If so, would you mind repeating it? If not, here's the way it works." I explain the test knowing that the candidate may be nervous about taking a personality inventory, and I always offer the assurance that there are no right or wrong answers.

I'm not as interested in the MBTI results, which identify a candidate as one of sixteen personality types, as I am in how long it takes to return the inventory, and how the person discusses the results, which we always do by phone or in a follow-up visit.

Let's say the new candidate is my type, identified in MBTI language as an INTJ—an Introverted (I), Intuitive (N), Thinking (T), and Judging (J) personality. This type has a few unflattering characteristics, such as praying earnestly, "Lord, keep me open to others' ideas, WRONG as they may be." Once an INTJ's mind is made up, usually quickly, it's like a bear trap closing. (This quality, unfortunately, describes me perfectly.) In our conversation afterward, the candidate has plenty of time to agree or disagree with the test results as it fits her personality. More significantly in terms of my task, does the candidate laugh? Does she elaborate on her independence? Her rigidities? Does she give examples? Do the results open up our discussion? Or does she clam up? Does the candidate think she can make an end run by saying, in all seriousness, as many candidates do, "Oh, I used to be like that, but I've really changed over the years."

There are two critical things to know about any psychological test. First, understand that an interpretation can be very insightful, neutral, or unhelpful. It all depends on the interpreter's expertise.

Second, tests are especially helpful when they correspond with a candidate's history, interview impressions, post-interview behavior, and reference checks. If they do, pay attention.

For example, on the Myers-Briggs Type Inventory, one description of a candidate included these phrases: "May become competitive and unappreciative of the input of others," and "May take criticism personally."

A second psychological evaluation of the same executive concluded, "He may tend to be blunt, fault-finding, and overly critical of others. He may sulk when not in the limelight."

A third interpreter, a handwriting analyst (see page 213) who didn't see the other results, said this about the candidate: "He is very sensitive to criticism and evaluation, even to the point of blowing it out of proportion. Under pressure the candidate is not beyond letting a sarcastic or angry remark fly."

Is this enough to eliminate the candidate? No. But an alarm should go off with corresponding results like these. Of course the candidate deserves an opportunity to respond to any problems that you put on the table.

Something else the handwriting expert wrote fit the candidate's post-interview behavior: "The candidate may tend to 'shoot himself in the foot' and subsequently resort to covering his tracks."

The man had been quite charming during the interview, but

afterward, when the selection process bogged down, he did let an angry remark fly and shoot himself in the foot. He called from an airport phone to vent his frustration. "I don't know what value your interview and tests have added to this process!" he blurted out. The next day he covered his tracks from another airport phone. "I didn't really mean that remark about you're not adding value. It's just that this process has been extraordinarily frustrating!"

Frustrating? If several psychological tests were frustrating, I couldn't imagine how a turnaround situation and a powerful chairman might push the man's hot buttons. On the other hand, psychological test results or not, the candidate had a twenty-year track record in North Carolina, and twenty years is infinitely more important than any and all interviewing and psychological testing.

So after the testing in the post-interview process, we found two highly reputable peers who had worked closely with the candidate for ten years in Chapel Hill, and whom he had not listed as references. Their independent comments were almost identical. "He's thin-skinned and can't get along with people, especially bosses and authority figures."

Although the search firm loved this man, I became the bearer of news that nobody wanted to hear. The man's interview and post-interview behavior, psychological tests, and reference information had all convinced me that this was the wrong candidate for the job, even if the search firm didn't believe it.

Strategy No.31:

Experiment with Handwriting Analysis

Like any filter, graphology is only as good as the expert interpreting the handwriting sample. Even then, it should be used only as an adjunct method. Such analysis is used by many businesses in Europe, as well as by the Mossad, the Israeli secret service.

It takes about ten minutes for a candidate to produce a handwriting sample. It can be done before, during, or after an interview. The candidate summarizes on one page why she would be a good person for the available job, and signs the page as she would sign a letter. The test is short, simple, inexpensive, and often revealing.

For example, George Soros is called "The World's Greatest Money Manager" and is one of the most influential investors in the world. According to one expert, Soros's writing is that of someone who is "very quick, representing a person who likes to be engaged. Also, he gambles on his passionate relationships, picking people from an intuitive, emotional response." Donna Karan is a fashion designer whose company racks up more than $400 million in annual sales. She has a remarkable instinct for what shoppers want, and her graphology report says, "The signature is highly original, though not legible. Legibility is not important here; style, flair, and expressiveness are." Have we learned anything new about George Soros and Donna Karan? Probably not, but if interpreted intelligently, handwriting analysis can reach well beyond a person's persona.

My own handwriting analyst of over twenty-five years wrote this of a particular candidate: "He has had some disappointment along the line, and he probably now puts his major effort into his work." When I discussed the results with the candidate, he was flabbergasted. He had just concluded a traumatic divorce, he told me, complete with dueling lawyers who took six months to settle just before the couple went to court. "So the analysis is right," he said. "I've put all my energies into work these past six months."

Another report warned me of a candidate: "Is he a dynamic person? No. Is he honest? Yes, but he is evasive by nature. Does he make decisions easily? No. He is bright, but not motivated. Strong, but not forceful. He does not come off as a highly committed or happy person." In this case the handwriting results dovetailed with the very strong intuitive reaction I had during a thirty-minute interview. However, the report wasn't discussed with the candidate in this case, because he did not have other overall strengths for the job in question.

Try this strategy, but don't rely on it. Consider negative results to be one of those flashing red lights. Move on, with caution, to the candidate's next play.

Contents: Chapter 4

Checking
References

"To paraphrase Winston Churchill, never, never, never, never compromise. The bad hire was a third choice after two others were not hired. I compromised because the search was taking inordinately long. My experience reminded me that no hire is better than a bad hire."

—John Armstrong, Vice President, News, Contra Costa Newspapers, Inc., Walnut Creek, California

Chapter 4: Checking References

A young *Washington Post* reporter named Janet Cooke created a false resume claiming that she was a graduate of Vassar College. Cooke later won a Pulitzer Prize when she wrote a fictitious story about an eight-year-old drug addict. According to *Time,* reference checking by employers increased as much as tenfold after Cooke was exposed.

The lesson is clear. When you're looking for demonstrations of a candidate in action, one of the most obvious places to turn is to the candidate's previous track record. If used correctly, references offer not only a snapshot of a person's life, but a photo album of strengths and limitations. Increasingly difficult to find in today's litigious climate, references also provide insight into a candidate's behavior.

Of course, we check references every day. If we're new to a neighborhood, we call other parents about potential babysitters for our children. We call for the names of honest mechanics or reliable dry cleaners in the area. But when it comes to hiring, especially if we fall in love during an interview, most of us balk at the next step. Not wanting to hear negative information, we have an allergic reaction to reference checking, and when we *do* force ourselves to do it, we have a tendency to confirm the *facts* rather than obtain *information.*

Anyone can give you facts. Few people give information. The key to checking references is to be motivated enough and persistent enough to keep calling people until you get meaningful information.

In *Information Anxiety,* Richard Saul Wurman gives a marvelous example of the difference between facts and information:

"Facts in themselves don't solve the problem. Facts are only meaningful when they relate to a concept that you can grasp. If I say an acre is 43,560 square feet, that is factual but it doesn't tell you what an acre is. On the other hand, if I tell you that an acre is about the size of an American football field without the end zones, it is not as accurate, but...I have made it infinitely more understandable to most Americans because it is as common a plot of ground as we have. We have a sense of that size. And you don't have to play football to know this."

Too often, reference checking is just fact checking and no more. For example, I received a call from a credit bureau in Michigan. My name had been given as a reference by Robin Bacci, a luxury car dealer applying for a new dealership. I was amazed by the brevity of our conversation. Did I know Robin? For how long? In what capacity? Did I have any negative information about her? Our conversation lasted less than thirty seconds, and during it I imagined the credit bureau employee, who probably made $8 an hour, going down a checklist of questions. A multimillion-dollar investment by Detroit was riding on our discussion, but the credit company's reference questions were rattled off as quickly as possible.

Is this story typical? I think so. Most people feel that checking references is about as appetizing as eating fish eyes. In addition, most human resources and legal departments are wary of litigation and advise their employees never to give out reference information except dates of employment. However, no one should ever hire without additional information. And if you get the human resources department or legal counsel on the phone in your search for information, you may as well cut short the interview.

On the other hand, if you're persistent, you'll eventually hit pay dirt. Persistence means more than just hanging in there. It means digging deeper—asking the candidate's references for other references, for example. Your patience will be rewarded, as themes, both positive and negative, emerge in the process. Persistence is a necessary ingredient of success.

Strategy No.32:

Ask the References to Call You Back

Here's the simplest, most effective reference check that I know. It's also fast and legal. Call references at what you assume will be their lunchtime—you want to reach an assistant or voice mail. If it's voice mail, leave a simple message. If it's an assistant, be sure that he or she understands the last sentence of your message. You say: "John (or Jane) Jones is a candidate for (the position) in our company. Your name has been given as a reference. *Please call me back if the candidate was outstanding.*"

The results are both immediate and revealing. If the candidate is outstanding or excellent, I guarantee that eight out of ten people will respond quickly and want to help. Take such a response as a green light. Proceed to the next level by checking out the individual.

However, if only two or three of the ten references selected by the candidate return your call, this message is also loud and clear. And yet:

☞ **No derogatory information has been shared.**

☞ **No libelous statements have been made.**

☞ **No confidences or laws have been broken.**

I know the owner of a family business who called ten references that a potential sales manager had given her, and when only two of the references returned her calls, she concluded, "I must have done something wrong." She thought the resounding silence was her fault!

Trust the results of this test. Asking references to return your call is an extraordinarily useful message. It's a strategy that requires minimal time and realizes maximum results.

Strategy No. 33:

Network Up the Chain of Command

References are often valuable in ascending order. Be persistent about moving up the chain of command. If necessary, discuss the candidate with people that you might know from industries and geographical locations listed on a candidate's resume.

For all references, the higher you go up an organization, the more likely you are to get helpful information.

Here's an example that is almost stranger than fiction. When I served on a school board several years ago, finding a new principal became our top priority, and the board of trustees formed a search committee. After interviewing candidates for over six months, a finalist was not just chosen, but ordained. The committee loved this man, loved his interviews, his charisma, and his charm. Our school board was expected to bless the coronation, but frankly, to one other board member and myself, this fellow seemed too good to be true. How does a fifty-year-old with twenty-five years in education at five different schools leave no footprints in the snow?

Seeing that the candidate had spent ten years as a school principal in Seattle, I called a good friend, Sam, who has a strong background in education in Seattle. I asked him to check the candidate out. Amazingly enough, Sam recognized the candidate's name immediately. Sam had actually served on this fellow's school board during his tenure in Seattle. According to Sam, one night the principal went, not to Portland as he told his wife and school board, but to rendezvous with a woman in suburban Seattle, and they were seen by another board member. The woman actually turned out to be a teacher at the school.

"What bothered me wasn't the affair," Sam concluded. "It was the principal's reaction to the questions posed to him by the school board in closed session. Not knowing that he had been observed, he lied about that night. When a forty-year-old principal lies to his school board, even after he's confronted with the truth in executive session, you're really in trouble. So we let him go. We bought out his contract and gave him a decent official recommendation. Then someone hired him in upstate New York. As he charmed your committee in San Francisco, I hear he wowed them in New York."

Without identifying Sam, I passed the story on to the search committee, which hated the message and basically shot the messenger. The school board ultimately rejected the candidate in a close vote, but the search committee chairman never spoke to me again.

How typical is this story? Very.

Unfortunately, an employer's ability to hear bad news about a potential employee is inversely proportional to the time spent courting that employee. Put another way, a person "in love" is almost always resistant to bad news.

Here's another example. A Silicon Valley investment company had bought 51 percent of a privately held, entrepreneurial business, expecting to harvest an enormous profit from an initial public offering scheduled for two years in the future. The company hired a search firm to come up with an appropriate executive to run their soon-to-be billion-dollar investment. Unfortunately, it took six months for the search firm to find a suitable candidate, who quickly met the key players, attended meetings, and visited stores.

The candidate made a terrific impression. The investment chairman likened the man's charm to "walking down the marriage aisle together. The more I interviewed him the more I liked him. I liked his energy, his people skills, and his questions." Three months into the courtship, the investment company was about to make the man an offer he couldn't refuse.

At the eleventh hour, the company's founder asked me what I thought. I thought: Here is another fifty-year-old male who casts no shadows.

Scanning the candidate's history, I saw that he had spent twenty years with a famous public corporation in Philadelphia. I didn't know the company's leadership, but luckily, I do have a friend who is a social friend of the chairman. I called her, and she called Philadelphia.

The executive told my friend that the candidate was good, but not as good as he thought he was. He is a political animal, the chairman said, and if he feels out of control he could be a "backstabber." His exact words. "I'll go on record," Mr. Philadelphia said in a rare display of candor. "I'd say this to the candidate's face."

Subsequently, the chairman did repeat his story to the investor, employing only slightly more diplomatic language. However, it was too late. The senior partner was ready for marriage and disregarded this flashing red light, which often happens when a search is taking inordinately long, and the candidate seems to be the best available. Under pressure, even the smartest people will start to rationalize that frogs really can turn into princes.

What happened?

Surprise, surprise. The candidate turned down the offer. Not only did he decline, he had his search firm decline for him, advising the investment firm that an Atlanta corporation had offered him more money and won the bidding war. The investors didn't even know there was a bidding war! They were furious. "We wasted three months," said one partner, "and the son-of-a-bitch never even called us."

As the French say, "The more things change, the more they stay the same." The "son-of-a-bitch" had only lived up to his reputation.

These two stories remind me of something a patient of mine once said about playing the messenger. "The truth will set you free," he told me. "Free from your friends, free from your relatives, free from almost everyone you know!"

Use the Internet as a Resource

It makes sense to research a person's record for half an hour in the library, or on the Internet, if the candidate has been active in his or her community. Unfortunately, that half an hour is rarely spent.

Bill Bidwell, the owner of the Phoenix Cardinals, could have saved himself a great deal of time and money if he had visited his local library before hiring Buddy Ryan as coach. Ryan's record wasn't a secret. In the library or via the Internet, Bidwell could have read that as the Chicago Bears' defensive coordinator, Ryan battled with head coach Mike Ditka during the Bears' Super Bowl season in 1985. From 1986 to 1990 he alienated Norman Braman, who'd hired Ryan to coach his Philadelphia Eagles, which lost in the first round of the playoffs for three straight years before Braman fired him. Absent from football during the next two years, Ryan made headlines again in 1993 when, as defense coordinator for the Houston Oilers, he punched offensive coordinator Kevin Gilbride in the jaw during a sideline altercation seen on national television. Presumably, Bill Bidwell knew this history. Yet despite it, he hired Ryan to coach the Phoenix Cardinals.

On arriving in Phoenix, Buddy Ryan announced, "You've got a winner in town," and he kept a sign on his desk that read, "If you ain't the lead dog, the scenery never changes." But slogans were no substitute for his past performance. After two losing seasons in Phoenix, Bidwell bought out the remaining two years of Ryan's contract in 1995 for $1.5 million. Trips to the Chicago, Philadelphia, and Houston libraries via the Internet would have been cheaper.

Here's another example. Walter J. Marks was hired as superintendent by the Kansas City school board in 1991. Available in libraries was the headline news that the Richmond Unified School District in California had agreed in December of 1990 to buy out the contract of superintendent Marks for $93,989 when the district's severe financial problems became apparent and eventually brought about its bankruptcy. Afterward a Richmond board member was quoted as saying, "I would have liked to out-and-out fire him without compensation. But we were told we could have ended up in court, spending more money than we had bought him out for." The same board member told a newspaper reporter that a Kansas City school trustee had called for a reference on Mr. Marks. "I told her as I saw it, and she said, 'My Lord, I wish we'd talked yesterday. We just hired him last night.'"

If the best predictor of future behavior is past behavior, history was about to repeat itself. As superintendent in Kansas City, Marks earned $140,000 a year until local television station KCTV aired a film of the superintendent in Florida on a paid medical leave, presumably recuperating from a chronic back problem. Yet the film showed Marks carrying lumber and moving large boxes. Marks was suspended in February of 1995.

How easy to use is the Internet? Very easy, even if you're a computer novice like me. If you don't have the equipment or time, the key is to find the right person to make the process painless, quick, and inexpensive. For a phone call, you can make a request and get results within hours. For example, I recently asked for some information on a man in Ohio, and a local research service used the Internet to get an enormous amount of public information, including newspaper articles, about the candidate. The cost of a half-hour search was $30; online database fees were $5; and sixteen pages of faxed materials were another $4. Was the six-figure candidate's public record worth the $39?

As they say in the Valley, *HELLO!*

Strategy No. 35:

Perform Due Diligence for All Finalists

Credit checks and investigative reports may have a part in reference checking, but you must check with an attorney beforehand. Few people tap the enormous wealth of publicly available data banks that may contain information on a candidate's driving and financial records, real estate dealings, court appearances, and litigation history. Perfectly legal, this is all public information and is readily available.

Credit Reports

A bad credit report may predict the future behavior of some candidates. These days a bad record can get you rejected for auto insurance in the United States. Some companies—Allstate for one—are more willing to sell auto insurance to a convicted speeder than to a person with a bad credit record. On the basis of statistical analysis, Allstate says that your credit rating is one of the best predictors of future claims on an auto policy.

I don't know about auto insurance, but how people handle credit and money, or the lack thereof, is a valid subject for discussion. Examine the situation carefully if the candidate is heavily in debt or overextended on credit card loans. But remember this caveat: Credit reports can be filled with misleading information.

According to *SmartMoney* magazine, one of the biggest credit-check companies in this country, Experian (once known as TRW), admits to handling 360,000 consumer complaints a month. Trans Union, another major credit report company, says that of the more than 2.5 million people who request its reports each year, 50 percent have a question or a dispute about their credit history.

One of my close friends applied for a mortgage loan and was rejected because he had been on a three-month sabbatical in France one summer. Unfortunately, his mortgage coupon had been lost in the mail between San Francisco and Paris. This blight on his perfect payment record showed up fifteen years after the fact.

My eldest daughter moved twice in one year while a student at Carnegie Mellon University in Pittsburgh, and a gas bill was never forwarded from Apartment #1 to Apartment #2. A red flag appeared on her credit report despite her explanation and the explanation of an attorney friend who called the credit company's legal counsel on my daughter's behalf.

The lesson is simple. Candidates deserve the chance to discuss their side of the story when it comes to credit checks and the reference reports you receive.

Investigative Reports

Is an investigator's report worth the expense? I think so with executive candidates. Although investigative services are commonly used for mergers, acquisitions, foreclosures, and divorce actions, these services can also be productive when hiring key personnel. For several hundred dollars, you can obtain a financial profile that includes, among other information, bank accounts, source of income, level of income, real property holdings, credit history and rating, litigation status (past and present), unsecured tax indices, motor vehicle record, watercraft/aircraft record, county records (tax liens, notices of default, etc.), and bankruptcies.

On pages 210–211 you'll find the names, addresses, and phone numbers of several companies that provide reputable credit and investigative services.

Strategy No.36:

Ask the Candidate, "What Will I Hear?"

Always ask the candidate, "What am I likely to hear—positive and negative—when I call your references?" The question is both practical and fair. Practical, because it allows the candidate to alert his references to your inquiry. Fair, because it tells the candidate that you will be checking his references in depth, and it gives him a chance to tell his side of the story.

A wise proverb says "He who lies on the ground cannot fall." I agree, and so do many others. Sometimes firms are distrustful of people who have never experienced failure. They want risk-takers, not people who play it safe. Some venture capitalists look on certain kinds of "failures" as a prerequisite for certain applicants. They think that the only real failure is the person who doesn't learn from his or her previous experiences.

Candidates always deserve the courtesy of explaining the peaks and valleys of their work history. Consequently, I like to ask, "What will I hear—positive and negative—when I call your references?" The results are fascinating. Here's the story of that graduate student whose resume appeared in Strategy 5(page 37).

Although his potential employer knew nothing about Japan, she asked the candidate, "What will I hear from your references?" The applicant said, "From Japan, you'll hear that I was a whistle-blower. From the American joint-venture partner, whom I didn't list as a reference, you'll probably hear me damned with faint praise." Then the interviewer asked the candidate for his side of the story.

In Japan, the young man had discovered that his boss was lying about the company's finances, sales results, and advertising expenditures. These problems aside, "Individuality does not exist in Japan," said the candidate. "Loyalty, a paramount cultural value, is to your boss, the group, and the company." Consequently, as a liaison between the joint-venture companies in America and Japan, the candidate's allegiance was divided. To what boss (and which country) should he tell the truth?

Never before had the young man faced this type of an ethical issue, nor was there a mentor with whom to discuss his boss's corruption. He raised the problems with his coworkers in Japan, but they were afraid. Their advice was to do nothing. In the end, however, he acted.

He called the American president of the joint-venture partner, a man with whom he had previously established a good relationship. Diplomatically, the candidate reported that the company was about to face some severe financial discrepancies and serious losses. Although the president seemed sympathetic, he made it clear that his primary loyalty was to the Japanese boss, someone he had dealt with for years. The president advised the young man that he should also remain loyal. The message the twenty-seven-year-old heard was that he had done the wrong thing by going over his boss's head. Devastated, the young man made preparations to leave Japan.

Then the floor caved in, the result of three years of financial cover-ups. His Japanese boss quit quite dramatically, and shortly after audits began to reveal the extent of his corruption: inaccurate sales figures, falsified advertising expenditures in the millions of dollars, and missing corporate funds. A lawsuit, an unheard-of option of in Japan, was being considered.

"What did I learn from the experience?" asked the candidate. "As a foreigner, I saw that Americans tend to invest in (and trust) Japanese, like my former boss, who speak adequate English. It's an understandable but often expensive mistake. On a more personal note, I also learned that I made the correct decision. By facing my fears and dealing directly with an ethical dilemma, I came to respect myself more."

After the candidate's story, the interviewer called references in Tokyo. The vice president of sales, who spoke excellent English because he had been raised in Australia, confirmed in detail the young man's story.

The Japanese vice president for finance, who was another reference, spoke no English, but used a local graduate student from a nearby university to translate. This reference had been with his company for thirty-three years. He also confirmed the young man's story through the translator. "He blew the whistle," said the manager, adding, "He saved our company."

By confronting adversity and telling the truth, the young man also got the job.

Strategy No.37:
Devise a Phone Reference Checklist

There are official and unofficial ways to check references. For phone conversations, I suggest that you devise a simple checklist such as one of the two prototypes below. Adapt them accordingly.

Here's one telephone model for reference checking suggested by Leon Farley, who leads his own search firm in San Francisco. He advises that you call and ask about:

1. Technical Competence

Can the candidate perform the required tasks? Can the university president raise money? Can the secretary spell? Can the receptionist handle phones? These are easy pitches, and references should be able to hit the ball out of the park.

2. Intelligence

This topic can take a few seconds to consider. "On a scale of one to ten, how would you rate the candidate's intelligence?" Most references respond well to a ten-point scale for rating people.

3. People Skills

Ask about the candidate's interpersonal skills. How does she get along with bosses? What about subordinates and peers? You'll usually get a ringing endorsement, but listen for silences, gaps, and omissions in this part of the conversation.

4. Motivation

What motivates the candidate? Financial rewards? Meaningful assignments? A job well done? Pats on the back? Independence? All of the above?

I have seen candidates decline offers because of relationships ("My fiance just accepted an offer in Salt Lake"), money ("My company just beat your offer"), and educational concerns ("My daughter's special school needs aren't available in your city"). How you structure your offer depends upon a person's motivations and your understanding of these motivations.

5. Everything Else

Finally you should say, "Is there anything that I haven't asked?" Then listen carefully.

Here's a second format for phone references, one originally developed by Charles Scott. ☞

Reference Questions

- Did you like the person?

- What did they fail at doing?

- Reputation in the company?

- How did they communicate?

- Reputation in the industry?

- How did they react to authority?

- Reason for leaving?

- Level of energy, drive?

- What did they accomplish?

- What would you change about the person if you could?

Examples of Experiences   **Role Person Played**

A. _____   _____

B. _____   _____

C. _____   _____

Regardless of format, it's critical that you listen carefully. It also helps to be a Type B personality who doesn't interrupt with "yeahs" and "uh-huhs." Here's a portion of a recent phone call I made. I had asked the reference to tell me about the pros and cons of the candidate. The conversation began:

"On the finance side, his skills are excellent."

(pause)

"He is very smart, very capable."

(longer pause)

"His difficulties are interpersonal..."

(longest pause)

"...and they're not insignificant."

I continued to listen without interrupting. The reference went on: "I hate to damn him, because I think that he is so capable. And if you have a person who can provide strong, hands-on supervision, maybe you can get excellent work from him."

The true feelings of most references are hidden between their words, inflections, pauses, and silences.

Meet References for the Finalists

The more personal your contact with the reference, the more likely you are to get honest information. Whenever appropriate, visit a key referral in their office to discuss a finalist candidate.

This strategy is as obvious as it is rare. If you have to drive across town or even fly across the country, your time will be well spent if the candidate proves an asset to your company. On the other hand, if your potential winner isn't outstanding, most reputable references will not want to look you in the eye. They will politely decline even a fifteen-minute face-to-face meeting in their office.

I recall a client who made ten phone calls to references before getting an appointment with a fellow who was willing to talk off the record. The candidate was a finalist for a critical position. My client had asked him, "Why are you leaving your current job?" Unpredictably, the candidate had replied that his Mormon boss, the chairman of a high-profile corporate chain, limited himself to Brigham Young graduates when he selected his key advisors. The candidate claimed he had been illegally excluded from the chairman's inner sanctum because of his religion; that's why his references had stonewalled by telephone until this one man had agreed to speak to my client.

After five minutes of pleasantries, the face-to-face meeting served its purpose. "The Mormon story is true," the reference confirmed. "And it's a shame, because the candidate is a real jewel. You'd be lucky to get him."

My client had hit the jackpot. This was the *information* he was looking for, deeper than data or facts he would turn up when checking references. He hired the candidate, to everyone's satisfaction. And no, the candidate never sued.

Contents: Chapter 5

Chapter 5

Final Strategies

"If each of us hires people who are smaller than we are, we shall become a company of dwarfs. But if each of us hires people who are bigger than we are, we shall become a company of giants."

—*David Ogilvy*, Ogilvy on Advertising

Chapter 5: Final Strategies

I think we can all agree that time is our most precious commodity. There aren't enough hours in the day. Final strategies aside, by now you're probably thinking, "Who's got time for three new ideas, let alone 200 plays?"

All of the hiring strategies presented in the preceding pages were designed to save time, not waste it, and to help us make the best possible choices. But there's no getting around it—those choices initially take time to make.

I like the story about the man in the rowboat, which illustrates the point. From the nearby shore, a woman sees the man in trouble. He's rowing like crazy, getting nowhere. Then she notices that the rowboat has a bad leak and is sinking. She shouts to the man, but he's too busy bailing and rowing to hear her. She continues to shout; he continues to row and bail like crazy. Finally she yells, "Hey, if you don't bring that boat ashore and repair the leak, you're going to drown!" The man replies, "Can't you see, lady, I DON'T HAVE TIME TO FIX THE DAMN LEAK."

The story reminds me that we all need to come ashore on occasion and fix our leaky boats. This is true at work and at home. Even if we don't have much time. Even without all the tools.

These last several strategies don't easily fit into the pre-interview, interview, or post-interview categories. They are a miscellaneous collection of related thoughts that I think you may find helpful.

Invest in People, Not Ideas

The secret in business today is not money or technology or ideas. It's people.

Howard Lester, the chairman and CEO of Williams-Sonoma, describes a deceptively obvious reason for a store's success.

"Look at your results," he says. "When a store consistently achieves a 20 percent–better result than the competition, including our own stores in similar cities, there's one reason. And it's not the demographics, local economics, smart marketing, or dumb luck. The secret is the store's manager." He goes on to describe a manager in Dallas who consistently produces results 20 percent higher than comparable Williams-Sonoma stores nationwide. In fact, when another store was down 20 percent, they moved that Dallas store manager to the troubled operation in Palo Alto, California. Whereas we might expect an enormous gulf between the Texas and California markets, we'd be wrong. The manager who achieved a 20 percent–better result in Dallas achieved the same in six months in Palo Alto.

"People are the secret," Howard Lester says. "It's so simple, no one believes it."

Arthur Rock, a venture capital legend associated with the formation of such companies as Intel, Apple, and Teledyne, put it more succinctly: "I invest in people, not ideas."

Hard to find? Absolutely.

Worth the effort? You bet.

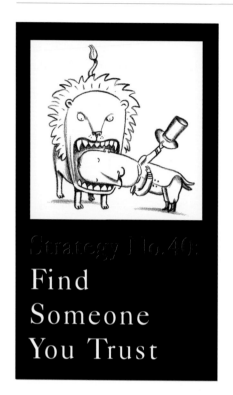

Strategy No. 40:

Find Someone You Trust

The higher up you progress in an organization, the more likely people are to protect you from bad news, including bad hires. Indeed, it's frequently hard to get the truth. It may be a way for the staff to ingratiate itself, or it may be what the leader truly wants. He or she may be conveying, consciously or unconsciously, "Don't bring me bad news." The previous sections have focused on the candidate and not factored into the equation the blind spots you may bring to the table.

In business, as in life, it helps enormously to have a colleague you can trust—or entrust—to tell you when you're making a mistake. When it comes to large corporations, small businesses, colleges, partnerships, and sports franchises, I have seen disastrous results when people agree with an executive who is dead wrong about a variety of issues, including the selection of key personnel—as the next story shows.

David R. Brown, president of Art Center College of Design, one of the world's premier design schools, got my name from a mutual friend. David called me on a Sunday morning at home. He had hired a new vice president three months earlier, and on Friday the VP's entire staff had threatened a mass resignation if the man wasn't let go immediately.

It sounded like a genuine emergency. So I scheduled individual, confidential interviews at Art Center on Wednesday.

I met David first. He is six feet eight inches tall and seems rather intimidating, although he is actually very shy. Then I met the vice president, who was as unhappy as the staff and felt like an outcast at the college. He knew the job wasn't working, but he wasn't prepared to resign.

Next I met the eight staff members, all affable, intelligent people, who were being driven crazy by the new man's arrogant attitude. Unfortunately, they were all so intimidated by David that they had not made their strong reservations about his choice for a VP known. Now their level of dissatisfaction had become so great that a mass resignation seemed the only dramatic way to get David's attention.

"Well, the issue is clear," I began at day's end in the president's office. "Do you want me to talk about the vice president—and I think you already know what you're going to do—or should we discuss the real problem?"

"What's that?" David asked.

"You," I said.

I half expected to be handed my head, but to my surprise, David settled back and listened intently as I gave him my impressions. He was the main asset and liability of Art Center, I said. Shouldn't we be asking why he picked the wrong person for the job in the first place?

David had been overwhelmed. He had needed help, and this man had great academic credentials. Hiring him seemed like a quick way of getting an extremely well-qualified candidate and immediate help. This was the problem, and we discussed it and possible solutions over the next hour.

Several weeks later, the vice president left with an appropriate settlement and his reputation intact. Since that memorable day David and I have become close friends, working together in various crises, and each of us trusts the other to tell the truth as he sees it. David has repeated the story of our first meeting more than once.

"Do you want to talk about the real problem?" he mimics me exactly. "Because it's you!" Then he leans back and roars with laughter.

Of course, David has also found someone on his staff who will challenge him when he's about to make the wrong decision, including hiring the wrong person.

The lesson is simple. We all make mistakes. But when no one tells the emperor that he has no clothes, neither the emperor nor the empire are well served.

(I asked David to read this section for accuracy. Instead, he read the entire book. He likes to say, "If I hadn't violated strategies 2, 4, 5, 6, 7, 8, 10, 13, 14, 15, 16, 17, 18, 20, 21, 25, 26, 28, 29, 30, 31, 32, 33, 35, 36, 38, and 42, things might have turned out differently!")

Follow These Three Cardinal Rules

At the end of the day, consult this checklist of cardinal rules. Consider the following when evaluating any candidate:

Honest:

Yes_____ No_____

Do you trust the candidate? If so, proceed to the next step. If not, stop here.

Clean Record on Crime and Alcohol:

Yes_____ No_____

Your call, but this question should appear on your radar screen. And consult your lawyer before you ask. For example, you can ask about felony convictions, but not about arrests. Legally, it's important to stick to public records here.

Physical Health:

Yes_____ No_____

Should health be on your radar screen? Again, it's your call, and you'll need an attorney's advice as to how you may or may not approach this subject. However, I met one employer who required that all her employees be insured by a minimal $10,000 life insurance policy. Why? Because a physical exam, including blood and urine samples, was required for the insurance. She felt that requiring an insurance policy was a quick, legal, and practical way to deal with her small business's soaring medical premiums.

Ask Yourself These Ten Questions

Here are ten quick questions from ten thoughtful people.

Your answer to each will reveal what you value in an employee.

1. Do you agree with Shakespeare's "Let's kill all the lawyers!"?

Check the public record in geographical locations where the candidate has lived and worked. If the candidate has been a repeated plaintiff in lawsuits, you should investigate further. And if rules are important, check with the local department of motor vehicles, which may make some of its records available to the public. If the candidate has twenty unpaid speeding tickets, it's thumbs down.

2. Do clothes make the man or woman?

Tell the candidate to come "informally" to the interview and see how *informal* is interpreted. Shorts and a Hawaiian shirt? (This actually happened, and not in Hawaii.) A three-piece suit and vest? (This also happened.) Whereas clothes don't necessarily make the man or woman, they do say something about the candidate.

3. Are drug-free employees important?

If so, require a drug-screening test of all applicants. There are different laws in different states, and it's important to understand the pros, cons, legalities, and limitations of drug screening, as well as the costs and percentages of false positives. (See pages 211–212 for two reputable labs and a reference who's willing to discuss a drug-free work environment with you.)

4. Does responsiveness count?

Send the finalist candidate written materials, videotapes, or Web site information. When you call two days later, has the candidate read (seen, digested, understood) the material? Does she have questions? If so, great. If not, rethink the candidate's suitability.

5. Should you create a model for future hires?

Give a battery of psychological tests to your best and worst employees. Do they fit any patterns? Use the best of these as models for future hires. Update frequently. Or follow Doubletree's lead. They have conducted interviews with 300 employees to analyze the personal attributes of standouts and washouts. (The employees don't find out which category they fall into.) Doubletree uses the results to create a database of "dimensions" for success and to search for people who fit the dimensions.

6. Do people like working for your candidate?

Contact the people who currently work for him—secretaries and administrative assistants, direct reports and coworkers. Do they revere the candidate? Or do they fear or resent him? All employees, past and present, can help predict future behavior.

7. Can your current employees help you?

Reward employees ($200 to $2,000) if they recommend a candidate you go on to hire. For example, Quad Graphics (as of 1997) employed 8,416 people. Of that total, 4,848 were related by blood or marriage—that was almost 60 percent of Quad's workforce!

8. Is documentation important?

If so, put all job offers in writing. It can help you and the candidates have a clear understanding of the position and your expectations. Include salary, job responsibilities, and title. Consult your attorney for appropriate language.

9. Do you also evaluate search firms, suppliers, and vendors?

If so, adapt appropriate strategies from these pages, especially from Checking References (pages 119–145), to select the best people available outside your organization.

10. When you add one new idea from this book, should you discard one old habit?

Yes. Otherwise, you'll just be adding to a full plate. Add new tools and subtract hiring practices that are outdated and time-consuming.

Strategy No. 42:

Use Yourself as a Test Case with Experts

Is the person I'm seeing the person I'm getting, or am I being conned by a great interview and interviewee? To answer, I suggest that you experiment on yourself with the experts and resources listed on pages 210–213. Once you get over the embarrassment, I can almost guarantee that you'll use this strategy on future candidates.

Let's say that you're interested in checking a candidate's public records, which you know are available through the Internet or via commercial services. Ask for your own public record: driving, mortgage, and credit history, litigation record, court proceedings, whatever. See what you think. Or, using yourself as a guinea pig, take a psychological test or submit a handwriting sample for analysis. Is the analysis accurate? Helpful? If so, experiment with a few candidates and select your experts based on their insights. If it's not helpful or cost-effective for whatever reason, toss it.

Such a test or tests may run about $300, but that's considerably cheaper than hours and hours of time-consuming interviews. Besides, if these services do work for you, you'll find them wonderfully simple tools for checking on a person's behavior.

Suggest a Trial Run When Possible

If you're still undecided about a person, give the candidate a longer assignment or hire a candidate on a temporary basis if it's practical. This can be anyone from an entry-level assistant to a senior executive. Watch the person under game conditions. Best behavior aside, red and green lights will become clearer during these auditions.

When my youngest daughter, Mara, was twenty-three years old, she was hired on trial for four months as a copy kid at a major daily newspaper. Her duties were to deliver papers at 7:00 A.M., answer phones for reporters, and sort mail. Her shift was specified to be seven and one-half hours, but often the office manager called at the last minute to ask if she could work a graveyard shift or double shift. Although the paper clearly lacked organization, those last-minute calls also tested how dedicated my daughter was to the job, even though her work was pretty mindless.

When Mara got off her shift, she made it a point to talk with the paper's editors. Relationships aside, what could she learn? And by the end of the first month, these same editors were sending her out to cover small press conferences. In addition, on her own time, with her own ideas, she soon began writing articles for the features section. Occasionally these articles ran. Often they didn't. But she went over the stories with an editor so that she could learn about the newspaper business and demonstrate her willingness to work eighteen hours a day.

After four months, Mara was given a full-time job and assigned to the women's page as an editorial assistant. She began writing stories, handling photos, and designing layouts—a huge step from sorting mail!

The office manager told my daughter that she remembered the first day Mara came to interview at the paper. They had been in a crisis and asked if she could start work that day. Although my daughter had an airplane reservation to go back to California that night, she canceled it to accommodate the paper. Even though they weren't offering Mara *a real job,* the office manager said, "That's when I knew you would make it."

Design Your Own Hiring System

At the end of my annual seminar for executives I always ask, "What tool(s) will you be able to use tomorrow? What are your best take-away ideas?" If I have thirty partici-pants, there will be at least twenty-five different answers that reflect the diversity of the group.

From the Summary Chart for Hiring Smart on pages 171–183, choose three or more that most appeal to you and design your own system around them.

Your Favorite Strategies:

1.

2.

3.

Other Strategies That Will Work:

4.

5.

6.

The General Manager Selection System

The chart on the next page comes from the American Golf Corporation (AGC), which operates more than 250 golf courses throughout America and Europe. Although the flowchart looks simple, it wasn't simple to produce. It took six months to hammer out, and it met with predictable resistance within the organization.

Nevertheless, there's a lesson here. The AGC flowchart is a good example of one picture being worth a thousand words. This single page summarizes an immensely effective selection process.

AGC used four pre-interview strategies, among others, that were appropriate for their business and came from the pages you've just read.

☛ **Applicants write a cover letter with their resume.**

☛ **Teams read resumes. To AGC's surprise, this change proved to be a time-saver instead of a time-waster.**

☛ **A terrific person with the gift of intuition was hired to do the company's initial phone screening since phone interviews proved a key to the new strategy.**

☛ **Finalists were asked to do a pre-interview assignment to demonstrate their written communication skills.**

Hiring smart instead of managing tough, AGC saved millions of dollars and an enormous amount of time and energy in the subsequent years. Therefore, I suggest one final strategy: *Design an appropriate flowchart on a single page that summarizes the best hiring strategies for your business.*

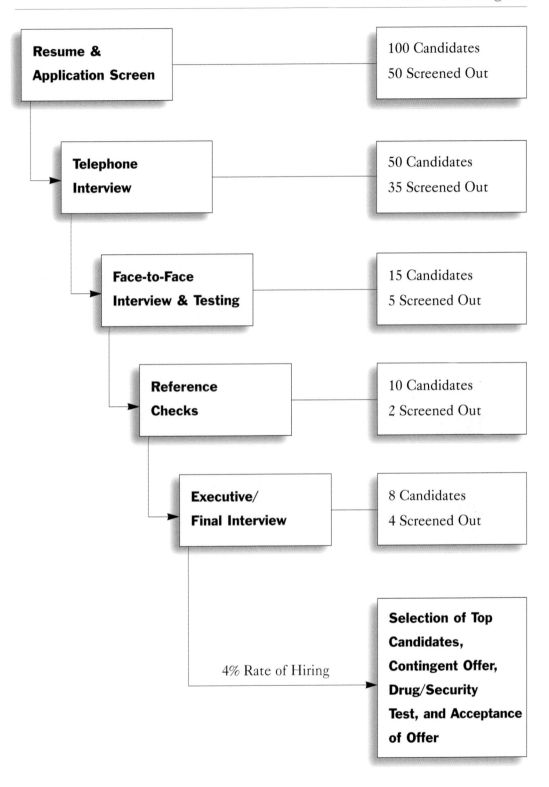

Resume &
Application Screen

100 Candidates
50 Screened Out

Telephone
Interview

50 Candidates
35 Screened Out

Face-to-Face
Interview & Testing

15 Candidates
5 Screened Out

Reference
Checks

10 Candidates
2 Screened Out

Executive/
Final Interview

8 Candidates
4 Screened Out

4% Rate of Hiring

Selection of Top
Candidates,
Contingent Offer,
Drug/Security
Test, and Acceptance
of Offer

"I brainwash myself with a scene. I go through each one 200 times.

—Anthony Hopkins, Academy Award Winner

Conclusion

Times change, but basic principles don't. And times are certainly changing. Downsizing is now called "involuntary separation from payroll" (Bell Labs), or "release of resources" (Bank of America), or "strengthening global effectiveness" (Procter & Gamble).

In a bizarre twist, Main Street's pain is Wall Street's gain. CEOs now earn 225 times the average worker's salary, up from forty-two times that salary only twenty years ago. In their "Force Management Program," AT&T announced another 40,000 layoffs, or 13 percent of Ma Bell's entire staff. The day after that carnage, AT&T's stock gained $10 billion in market value. Obviously, the implied promise of lifetime job security in exchange for hard work and loyalty no longer exists. When AT&T's exchairman Robert Allen announced the massive downsizing of his company, the joke that went around the office was that AT&T stood for "Allen and two temps." As one observer of this bloodbath said, "We are all temps."

Of course, there's another story being written today. There are 18,000 unfilled positions in Silicon Valley. High-tech companies in Austin, Texas, say they want to add 15,000 people this year. Last year Boeing hired an astounding 20,000 employees, sometimes as many as 500 people in a single week.

All this makes your hiring choices so much more critical. Whether the job front shrinks or expands, there's less room for error, and every new hire counts. In a rising or falling economy, the lesson is the same. The cost of bringing the wrong person on board is often enormous.

On the other hand, the most successful hiring system will be one that suits *your* style. Dee Hock, who founded and led VISA to astronomical growth (about 10,000 percent), articulates what guided his system:

"Hire and promote first on the basis of integrity; second, motivation; third, capacity; fourth, understanding; fifth, knowledge; and last and least, experience. Without integrity, motivation is dangerous; without motivation, capacity is impotent; without capacity, understanding is limited; without understanding, knowledge is meaningless; without knowledge, experience is blind. Experience is easy to provide and quickly put to good use by people with the other qualities."

So experiment. As my friend Howard Stevenson says, "No success is forever and no failure is final." Remember that Thomas Edison, Jonas Salk, and all the giant contributors to the way we experience life today spent about 98 percent of their time investigating the things that didn't work before they found what did. Put another way: Success in hiring represents the 2 percent that results from the 98 that is so-called failure. Success is achieved only through patience and practice.

Is it worth the time to find great players? Yes. Nothing you do at work is more important than selecting the right people. No matter how times change, this principle never will. At least I hope it won't. Hiring smart comes back tenfold to every organization that I know.

One final note. The strategies in this book evolved with the invaluable input of the many clients and friends with whom I have worked. I can only hope that such feedback will continue from readers. I'm especially interested in techniques or tests that have worked for you that have not been mentioned in this book.

Your comments would be much appreciated and can be sent to me at the following address:

Pierre Mornell

1 Park Avenue

Mill Valley, CA 94941

or via my Web site: www.hiringsmart.com

Many thanks, and good luck.

"The real challenge is to make good communication a handy and well-used tool. Then you are likely to pick it up and use it without thinking.**"**

—*Max DePree*, Leadership Is an Art

Summary Chart for Hiring Smart

'm convinced that what people in business today need are practical tools, not more theories. The strategies on the previous pages are designed to be user-friendly, and this summary chart should act like a toolbox. Eventually, I hope, you'll pick up these handy tools and use them without thinking.

Strategy	Benefit
1. Make Phone Contact Before the initial interview, pick up the phone and call the candidate. Whether you're the president of a company interviewing your prospective assistant or the manager of an ad agency interviewing an incoming creative talent, place the phone call yourself.	First impressions, even by phone, can tell you a lot about a candidate.
2. Ask for a Letter & Resume If appropriate, regardless of the material already in your file, ask the candidate to send a resume with a one-page cover letter that briefly highlights his or her life and background. This can be requested in your initial phone call.	Answers several questions immediately. Is the candidate prompt or slow, literate or illiterate, sloppy or neat, able to follow directions or not?

Strategy	Benefit
3. Give an Assignment	
Ask the candidate to visit one of your stores, plants, campuses, offices, or your Web page before the interview. Then ask for the candidate's observations.	Shifts the 800-pound hiring gorilla from the interviewer to the interviewee.
4. Walk Around the Office	
Help the candidate relax by walking around the office. These few minutes are a terrific opportunity to make small talk and lower anxieties. Look for curiosity — does the candidate ask questions? What other behavior does the candidate exhibit?	Sets the stage for a productive interview, while providing additional insight into the candidate's skills.
5. Read Resumes in Teams	
It's helpful—and faster—to read the top candidates' resumes in teams of three to five people. Watch for one of your team members to emerge, eventually and unpredictably, as your in-house resume expert.	Teams are more accurate and insightful about resumes than are many individual readers.

Strategy	Benefit
6. Cast the Widest Net	
Let a wide range of people know that you're looking for excellent candidates. Use the Internet and college career centers. In addition, keep data banks of excellent candidates who elect to work elsewhere.	With a better candidate pool, you're sure to have better finalists.
7. Use Caution with Big Changes	
Hiring people from big companies to little companies, top-down to bottom-up organizations, or structured to entrepreneurial settings, can be dangerous.	Helps you recognize that 300-pound defensive linemen don't make great quarterbacks, and vice versa.
8. Rethink the Position	
Before interviewing new candidates for old jobs, it's an excellent time to rethink the job itself.	Improves the efficiency of your organization.
9. Pre-Interview Combinations	
Integrate several of the preceding strategies into your hiring system in order to cut down on the number of interviews required to fill the position.	Saves hours, even days, of your time.

Strategy	Benefit
10. Pre-Interview Interview	
Keep your initial interview short. Although brief meetings are not always practical, they will save more time and energy than you can imagine.	Short interviews are especially helpful with candidates who look good on a resume, but who are less impressive in person.
11. Trust Your Instincts	
When selecting people, chemistry is crucial. It's either good, bad, or absent. Chemistry is usually determined in the first few minutes of an interview. Where chemistry is important and it's bad or nonexistent, cut the interview short.	Another time-saving device that streamlines the hiring process.
12. The Passionate Candidate	
The passionate candidate will love his job. The passionate candidate is dedicated. The passionate candidate will work hard. When passion is present, the sky is the limit. When passion is missing, all bets are off.	Provides a window into the future performance of a candidate.
13. All Your Questions at Once	
As the official interview commences, ask all your questions at once.	You avoid talking too much, which frees you to listen.

Strategy	Benefit
14. Have Fun	
Pick two or three "Columbo-type" questions and enjoy yourself.	If you're relaxed and having fun in an interview, the candidate should respond accordingly, and you'll learn a good deal in the process.
15. Assign a Mini-Project	
Three quarters of the way through the interview, give the candidate a task to perform.	Demonstrates the candidate's work behavior, while breaking the monotony of most interviews.
16. Seek Closure	
"We have about five more minutes…" is a useful statement before closure. Pay attention to "By the way…," "Oh, one more thing…," and "I almost forgot…," which mean, "This is the most important thing I'm going to say."	Candidates invariably say something that's really important at the end of the interview, regardless of the time you've already spent together.
17. Inappropriate Behavior	
Pay attention to a candidate's behavior, not words, especially if you can't explain the candidate's behavior during the selection process.	Enables you to isolate issues that don't come out through verbiage.

Strategy	Benefit
18. Strengths & Weaknesses	
No one is good at everything. We play to our strengths. But the reality is that our strengths, in the extreme, may predict our weaknesses. If a candidate says, "I'm great with the big picture," you should think, "What about the details?" True of all candidates.	Reveals strengths and hints at what might exist on the other side of the looking glass.
19. Be the Expert	
The rule of thumb is: If a candidate can go into detail and depth about a subject, he probably has some expertise in that area. If not, the opposite is true. On the other hand, the key is to ask questions in your areas of expertise.	Places you on firmer ground in evaluating a candidate's responses.
20. Take Notes	
Use a pad with a line drawn down the middle. On one side of the page, make appropriate notes about what the candidate tells you regarding jobs, dates, strengths, weaknesses, etc. On the other side, note what you're thinking.	After the interview, both sides of your pad will be influential in your decision.

Strategy	Benefit
21. Interview in Teams	
Interviewing in teams is a rare, but more thorough means of evaluating candidates.	As with team resume reading, this strategy provides more input and can yield more insights.
22. Ask for a Legal Release	
Have the candidate sign whatever releases are relevant. Check with your legal counsel to adapt generic releases to your business or organization.	Cuts down on costly litigation.
23. Throw a Few Curveballs	
Do something unpredictable after the interview, like walking the candidate to his car. Note make, model, location, and anything else that says something personal about the candidate. Look for surprises.	Another strategy aimed at revealing all the dimensions of a candidate.
24. Ask for a Return Call	
Before a candidate leaves my office I make a simple request: "Please call me back on Monday." It's an easy way to observe behavior.	Tells you if a candidate meets a time obligation. (Ten percent will miss the call back!) It's another way of passing that 800-pound hiring gorilla over to the candidate.
25. Assign a Take-Home Project	
Give the finalist candidates a current project you're evaluating and ask them for an analysis.	Evaluates attention to detail, as well as an ability to analyze problems and suggest solutions.

Strategy	Benefit
26. Travel with Finalists	
If one picture is worth a thousand words, then one trip is worth a hundred interviews.	Lets you observe the candidate under game conditions.
27. Meet the Spouse	
If you're seriously interested in an executive candidate, always meet the candidate's spouse or partner, if they have one.	The spouse or significant other is, after all, a key person without whose support even great hires are doomed to failure.
28. Put Problems on the Table	
If you're still interested in the candidate, always have a final interview in which you talk about potential problems. It's never a question of *if* problems will arise on a new job, but *what* those problems will be.	It's a plain reality that problems will arise. This gives you and your prospective hire a head start on possible solutions.
29. Use an Intuitive Person	
Use a person with the gift of intuition to help in the selection process. This may be a spouse, a board member, a receptionist, or a friend.	Utilizing various sources of information provides different perspectives on the candidate and helps predict future job performance.

Strategy	Benefit
30. Psychological Tests	
I like to give prospective employees a fifteen-minute psychological inventory, which I ask them to return by mail or fax the next morning.	Test results may converge on a potential problem.
31. Handwriting Analysis	
Like any filter, graphology is only as good as the expert interpreting the handwriting sample. (Even then, it should be used only as an adjunct method.)	An analysis is short, simple, inexpensive, and often revealing.
32. Ask for a Call Back	
Call references at what you assume will be their lunchtime—you want to reach an assistant or voice mail. If it's voice mail, leave a simple message. If it's an assistant, be sure that they understand the last sentence of your message. You say: "John (or Jane) Jones is a candidate for (the position) in our company. Your name has been given as a reference. *Please call me back if the candidate was outstanding.*"	The simplest, most effective reference check I know.

Strategy	Benefit
33. Network Up	
References are valuable in ascending order. Be persistent about moving up the chain of command. If necessary, discuss the candidate with people that you might know from industries and geographical locations listed on a candidate's resume.	The higher you go in an organization, the more you're likely to learn.
34. Use the Internet	
It makes sense to research a person's record for half an hour in the library, or on the Internet, if the candidate has been active in his or her community.	It helps to know a person's public record, as past behavior is a good indicator of future behavior.
35. Perform Due Diligence	
Credit checks and investigative reports may have a part in reference checking, but you must check with an attorney beforehand. Few people tap the enormous wealth of publicly available data banks that exist today.	How a person handles credit and other important aspects of life may help to predict future behavior.

Strategy	Benefit
36. Ask, "What Will I Hear?"	
Always ask the candidate, "What am I likely to hear—positive and negative—when I call your references?"	Informs applicants you'll be checking references and gives them a chance to tell their side of the story. Adds to the information you've gathered in the interview.
37. Devise a Phone Checklist	
There are official and unofficial ways to check references. For phone conversations, I suggest that you devise a simple checklist.	It's easy to use.
38. Meet References	
The more personal your contact with the reference, the more likely you are to get honest information. Whenever appropriate, visit a key referral in their office to discuss a finalist candidate.	Face-to-face meetings are superior to phone conversations, especially for top-level prospects.
39. Invest in People	
The secret in business today is not money or technology or ideas. It's people.	When you invest in the right people, you'll see measurable results.

Strategy	Benefit
40. Find Someone You Trust	
The previous sections have focused on the candidate and not factored into the equation the blind spots you may bring to the table.	Reminds you not to believe your own public relations.
41. Three Cardinal Rules	
At the end of the day you need a short list of cardinal rules. Go against these principles at your own peril.	Reminds you not to overlook your own intuition, as well as the candidate's history.
42. Ask Yourself Ten Questions	
Your answer to each will reveal what you value in an employee.	Adds to your arsenal of better ways to select and hire the right people.
43. Use Yourself as a Test Case	
Experiment on yourself with the experts and resources in Nuts and Bolts. Once you get over the embarrassment, I can almost guarantee that you'll use this strategy on future candidates.	A taste test: If you're impressed, you'll serve it to others.

Strategy	Benefit
44. Suggest a Trial Run	
If you're still undecided, give the person a longer assignment or hire a candidate on a temporary basis if it's practical. This can be anyone from an entry-level assistant to a senior executive.	Enables you to watch an individual under game conditions. Best behavior aside, red and green lights will become clearer during these auditions.
45. Design Your Own System	
Look over the previous forty-four strategies. Pick out your favorite three and incorporate these ideas into your hiring process.	Incorporating several strategies into a personalized hiring plan will save time, money, and energy on your next hire. It will also raise the bar on better applicants and ensure better finalists.

"...no one achieves a house by blueprints alone, no matter how accurate or detailed. A time comes when one must take up hammer and nails."

—*Allen Wheelis, How People Change*

Nuts & Bolts

This section includes a variety of practical information and suggests a logical sequence for an interview. It answers the questions: What are some good interview questions? How do I have more fun with candidates? What's legal to ask about? What's not legal? It also includes a resource guide to credit services, investigative services, drug testing, handwriting analysis, and behavioral testing.

The Ten-Step Interview

1. Make small talk.

2. Go over the job briefly.

3. Ask questions in sequence.

   a. education

   b. job history

   c. outside interests

   d. strengths

   e. shortcomings

   f. goals, personal and professional

4. Take notes.

5. Probe, probe, probe—always in your areas of expertise!

6. Announce, "We have about five more minutes."

Then listen carefully. ☞

7.   Tell the candidate what to expect next in the selection

     process and when.

8.   Let the candidate ask questions.

9.   Thank the candidate.

10. Compare notes with other interviewers.

Interview Questions

The following are representative interview questions that have been suggested to me. Always remember that questions must be job related unless the candidate initiates the subject.

- If you had only one word to describe yourself, what would that be?

- What is the most important thing you contribute to any organization?

- What are your goals, personal and professional?

- If you get the job, how could you lose money for me?

- What is your favorite book?

- What is your favorite movie?

- What is your favorite Web site?

- How do you deal with stress or conflict? What are the clues you have come to recognize that signal you are under too much stress?

- Discuss your parents' philosophy and the values they taught you. How are you similar to each of them? How are you different from each of them?

- Describe your personality.

- What are your major strengths and weaknesses?

- What do your bosses, peers, and subordinates say about you?

- What are the things that bother you most about people?

- Describe your current position and responsibilities.

- What skills do you need to fulfill these responsibilities successfully?

- Name three things you like and dislike about your current position. What would you change about your current job?

- I've never really understood the_____department very well. What do they really do? (A Columbo-type question.)

- When have you failed? Describe the circumstances and how you dealt with and learned from the experience.

- What would you like to do better? How are you managing this self-improvement program?

- What would you say about your organizational abilities? For example, how do you organize your day, week, etc.?

- If you're neat and orderly in your work life, where are you "wild and crazy" in your personal life?

- What percentage of your time do you spend in the following areas:
  - **a.** planning (long-range and short-term)
  - **b.** meetings
  - **c.** managing people
  - **d.** telephone
  - **e.** written communications
  - **f.** decision making

- If you had no economic or practical considerations and you could have any job or jobs you wanted, what would they be and why?

- How do you spend your time outside of work?

- How would you choose to spend additional time if you had it?

- Give me a list of "I likes," both personal and professional.

- What kind of books do you read? Tell me about the most recent books you've read.

- What was the best job you ever had, and why?

- What chores or responsibilities do you dislike the most?

- What qualities or characteristics do you believe limit or could limit you from reaching your desired career potential?

- Identify one event that has frustrated your career growth.

- Have you ever been terminated from a job? What were the reasons?

- In considering a new position what do you look for? What are the five most important features for you in a job?

- How are you unique?

- What changes have you made in your approach to others in order to become more accepted in your work environment?

- What are some examples of your ability to manage and supervise others? Give specifics of people who have grown as a result of your influence.

- In your previous positions, what kind of pressure did you encounter?

- What kind of people do you find it most difficult to work with?

- What kind of people do you work with best?

- Are there any talents you possess that are used during your leisure time that you have not been able to apply in a work situation?

- Describe a difficult obstacle you have had to overcome. How did you handle it? How do you feel this experience affected your personality or abilities?

- Who are some of your heroes?

- What are your long-term career objectives?

- Who or what in your life has influenced you most with regard to your career objectives?

- What do you think are the most important characteristics and abilities for any person's success? How do you rate yourself in these areas?

- What do you think are the most important characteristics of the manager of the future?

- Give examples of important decisions you have made that affected the bottom line of the business. Describe in detail the process you went through to make these decisions. What were the results?

- What decisions have you made that were incorrect and cost the company money? Explain.

- Who do you turn to for help when making decisions?

- What work environment is optimal for your satisfaction and performance?

- Is there any question I haven't asked you that I should?

- What questions do you have for me?

- What would you do if you won the lottery?

Word Pictures and Puzzles

To see if a person can visualize problems in new ways, try these six puzzles. The answers follow.

Puzzle #1:

A man gets out of jail and pushes his car to a nearby hotel, where he leaves a considerable sum of money. Next he pushes his car to a nearby house, where he leaves less money. What's going on here?

Puzzle #2:

Ferdy and Gerdy are going down the highway in their car and run out of gas. Ferdy remembers an exit a few miles back and says he'll go for gas. "But," he tells Gerdy, "lock the doors and roll up the windows. It's a dangerous world and there are lots of crazies out there." Gerdy says she understands and will lock the car.

Ferdy comes back an hour later with the gas. As he approaches, he sees a highway patrol car and a policeman peeking in his car. All the doors and windows are locked, but they see through the window that Gerdy has passed out, and a stranger is next to her.

As Ferdy puts the key in the door and unlocks the car, the policeman knows who the stranger is, how he got in, what happened, and that no crime had been committed.

What does the policeman know?

Puzzle #3:

Henry's mother, Mabel, has four children, that is all.

The first one's name is "Summer," the second one's name is "Fall."

"Winter" is the third one, and that leaves one more.

Can you guess the name of the final babe she bore?

Puzzle #4:

A night watchman hears a man yelling through a closed door, "Don't shoot me, Frank!" Then the night watchman hears a "Bang! Bang!" He opens the door and comes into the room, where there is a doctor, a lawyer, and a plumber, as well as a dead man and the gun that murdered him. He's never seen the suspects before, but he says, "I'm arresting you for this murder." And he arrests...the plumber. How did he know who did it?

Puzzle #5:

A deaf mute goes to a token booth in a subway station. He hands the token seller a dollar. Tokens are forty cents each. She hands him two tokens and twenty cents in change. No words or gestures or written communication takes place. How did the token seller know the deaf mute wanted not one, but two tokens (plus change)?

Puzzle #6:

A man is running home. Another man with a mask jumps out at him, and the first man turns around and runs in the opposite direction. Why? What kind of mask? Who are the men? What am I talking about?

Puzzle Answers

Puzzle #1:

He's playing Monopoly.

Puzzle #2:

Gerdy had a baby.

Puzzle #3:

Henry.

Puzzle #4:

He sees the doctor and lawyer are women.

Puzzle #5:

He handed her four quarters.

Puzzle #6:

They're playing baseball. The runner rounds third base and heads for home when the catcher (with his mask) blocks home plate.

Ten Curveballs

1. Ask three questions at once. See if the candidate remembers the questions without reminders.

2. Ask a question in the middle of the interview, and then remain silent.

3. Give conflicting opinions early in the interview. Then see if the candidate agrees with both opinions throughout the interview.

4. Take candidates out for coffee, lunch, etc., but let them drive their own cars. Slow? Fast? What are the candidate's driving habits?

5. Ask candidates what kind of bumper sticker they have on their car.

6. Ask the candidate a public record question to which you already know the answer—motor vehicle violations, litigation history, etc.

7. Try Henry's Ford's trick: Take the candidate to lunch and see if he salts the food before tasting it.

8. Ask, "How are you going to lose money for me?" (The question is really: "Where have you made mistakes before? Where might you make mistakes again?")

9. For sales people, ask the candidate to "call me early next week." See what the candidate thinks "early" means. Hopefully, it's first thing Monday morning. Even so, one employer suggests that you don't return the call, especially if the candidate is applying for a sales position. See if the candidate calls back until reaching you, preferably by Monday afternoon.

10. Ask, "Are you lucky?"

Sample Legal Release Forms

IMPORTANT NOTICE TO APPLICANT: PLEASE READ THESE NOTICES AND CONSENT FORMS VERY CAREFULLY BEFORE SIGNING.[1]

YOU WILL BE PROVIDED WITH A COPY OF THIS FORM AT ANY TIME UPON REQUEST

REQUEST, AUTHORIZATION, AND CONSENT FOR RELEASE OF INFORMATION TO EMPLOYER AND RELEASE FROM LIABILITY FOR DISCLOSURE OF INFORMATION

I understand that in connection with the application process, [INSERT COMPANY NAME] may request information from my past employers, educational institutions, personal references, and any public or private agencies that have issued me either a professional or vocational certification or license. I also understand that such investigation may include a review of any criminal records. I have provided complete and truthful information to [INSERT COMPANY NAME] regarding all sources of information about my past employment, education, licensure, certification, criminal conviction record, driving record, as well as any other information requested in the employment application, and am aware that any misrepresentations or material omissions concerning such information will be grounds for denying my application, withdrawing any offer of employment, or immediate discharge, regardless of when such misrepresentation or material omission is discovered. In order to assist [INSERT COMPANY NAME] in obtaining documents and information to confirm my background, if necessary, I hereby consent to the release of information more specifically described below.

A.   **Request, Authorization, and Consent to Release of Employment Information and Education Records**

I request, authorize, and consent to the release of information to [INSERT COMPANY NAME] regarding my previous employment and authorize all past employers or agents that they may designate, to respond to verbal or written inquiries from [INSERT COMPANY NAME] regarding my employment record, including, but not limited to, positions held, dates of employment, last pay rate, work performance,

---

[1]   This form is reprinted with the express permission of Littler Mendelson, a Professional Corporation. Any other reproduction or reprinting is prohibited. This form should be used only in consultation with legal counsel, as the law governing applicant background checks can be restrictive and complex.

disciplinary records, reliability, and any incidents of dishonesty, insubordination, violence, and/or unsafe, harmful or threatening behavior, including information based upon materials in my personnel files. I also request, authorize, and consent to the release and disclosure of educational records from any and all public or private educational institutions that I have attended to [INSERT COMPANY NAME], including all records of my academic performance, courses attended, grades earned, diplomas, degrees, or other certificates conferred.

B. **Request, Authorization, and Consent to Release of Personal Reference Information**

I request, authorize, and consent to [INSERT COMPANY NAME]'s contacting the personal references identified in my application for employment. I specifically request, authorize, and consent to [INSERT COMPANY NAME]'s verbal or written inquiries addressed to my personal references about the information contained in my application, as well as my reliability, honesty, and potential tendency, if any, to engage in any form of violence or other harmful, unsafe, or threatening behavior.

C. **Request, Authorization, and Consent to Release of Licensing or Certification Information**

I request, authorize, and consent to the release of information from any public agency or private entity concerning any professional or vocational license or certification that I have held in the past or currently hold, including, but not limited to, information concerning whether such license or certification is in good standing and any disciplinary or other proceedings concerning such license or certification.

D. **Request, Authorization, and Consent to Investigation of Criminal Records**

I request, authorize, and consent to [INSERT COMPANY NAME]'s thorough investigation of whether I have a record of criminal convictions, and if so, the nature of such criminal convictions and all surrounding circumstances available through lawful means. [INSERT COMPANY NAME] has advised me that its criminal background check will focus on convictions and that a criminal record will not necessarily disqualify me from employment.

RELEASE OF CLAIMS

I further hereby release and hold harmless [INSERT COMPANY NAME], its officers, employees, and agents, and any other person, or public or private entity inquiring about, investigating, furnishing, communicating, reviewing, or evaluating information or documents pursuant to this Request, Authorization, Consent and Release, or making any written or verbal communications for such purposes, from any and all claims arising from such activities, including, but not limited to, any claims whatsoever for defamation, fraud, misrepresentation, intentional or negligent interference with prospective business relations or contract, breach of contract (including any settlement agreement), negligent or intentional infliction of emotional distress, violations of applicable federal or state laws governing employee references and/or disclosure of employment information, and any other potential claims, demands, damages, liabilities, and/or actions of any kind whatsoever, whether known or unknown to me presently, that I may have, now or in the future.

I voluntarily grant this release for purposes of supporting my application for employment and based upon my desire to encourage [INSERT COMPANY NAME]'s consideration of my application. I understand that I may raise with [INSERT COMPANY NAME] any concerns I might have about the information that may be provided to [INSERT COMPANY NAME] during its investigation of my application.

I additionally agree to fully cooperate with [INSERT COMPANY NAME] in permitting the release of the above information and reports. I additionally understand that all information and documents generated, received, or maintained by [INSERT COMPANY NAME] during, or as a result of, its investigation, will be maintained as confidential information and that [INSERT COMPANY NAME] will not release such information or documents to me, except as otherwise required by applicable federal, state, or local law.

_____   _____
Date   Applicant Signature

_____   _____
Witness   Print Name

NOTICE AND CONSENT CONCERNING CONSUMER REPORTS
FOR EMPLOYMENT APPLICATIONS AND EMPLOYMENT PURPOSES [2]

This form, which you should read carefully, has been provided to you because [INSERT COMPANY NAME] may request consumer reports or investigative consumer reports in connection with your application for employment or during the course of your employment (if any), with [INSERT COMPANY NAME]. Any information contained in such reports may be taken into consideration in evaluating your suitability for employment, promotion, reassignment, or retention as an employee. Such reports, if obtained, will be prepared by a consumer reporting agency and may contain information concerning your credit standing or worthiness, character, general reputation, personal characteristics, or mode of living. The types of reports that may be requested include, but are not limited to, credit reports, criminal records checks, court records checks, and/or summaries of educational and employment records and histories. The information contained in such reports may be obtained from public record sources or through personal interviews with your neighbors, friends, associates, current or former employers, or other personal acquaintances.

If [INSERT COMPANY NAME] requests an investigative consumer report, which would include personal interviews as described above, you will receive a second notice indicating that the report has been requested no later than three days after the request is made to a consumer reporting agency. This additional notice, if issued, will advise you as to your further rights pertaining to investigative consumer reports.

If any adverse decision is made with regard to your application or employment (if any) based entirely or in part on the information contained in a consumer report, you will be notified as to the basis of that decision and given a copy of the report, as well as a summary of your applicable rights. If you have ever filed for bankruptcy, such information may or may not be relevant for employment purposes, but no employment decision will be based solely on this information.

Your consent is required by law before [INSERT COMPANY NAME] may obtain a consumer report or investigative consumer report pertaining to your potential employment or actual employment (if any) with [INSERT COMPANY NAME]. Your signature in the first space below indicates that you have carefully read and

---

2   This separate form is intended to comply with the federal Fair Credit Reporting Act, 15 USC § 1681 et seq., which applies to virtually all reports prepared by third party agencies regarding applicants and employees. Because the Act's requirements are rather complex, legal counsel should be consulted before using this separate form or requesting third party investigations of applicants or employees.

understand this notice and consent to the release of a consumer report or an investigative consumer report to [INSERT COMPANY NAME] for employment purposes, at [INSERT COMPANY NAME]'s discretion, either in connection with your job application, or in connection with any future decisions concerning your employment, promotion, reassignment, or retention as an employee of [INSERT COMPANY NAME], if any. Your signature additionally reflects your understanding that such consent will remain in effect indefinitely until you revoke it (cancel it) in writing, as described in the next paragraph.

CONSENT STATEMENT

I have carefully read and understand this notice and consent form and, by my signature below, consent to the release of consumer or investigative consumer reports, as defined above, to [INSERT COMPANY NAME] in conjunction with my application for employment. I further understand that this consent will apply during the course of my employment with [INSERT COMPANY NAME], should I obtain such employment, and that such consent will remain in effect until revoked in a written document signed by me. In the event that I wish to revoke this consent at any time, I understand that I may do so by either signing the Refusal or Revocation of Consent Statement below and returning it to [INSERT COMPANY NAME], at [ADDRESS] or sending a signed letter or statement to [INSERT COMPANY NAME] at the same address, indicating that I revoke my consent to [INSERT COMPANY NAME] obtaining consumer reports or investigative reports about me for employment purposes. I further understand that any and all information contained in my job application or otherwise disclosed to [INSERT COMPANY NAME] by me may be utilized for the purpose of obtaining the consumer reports or investigative consumer reports requested by [INSERT COMPANY NAME] and confirm that all such information is true and correct.

_____

Name of Applicant or Employee (Printed)   Social Security Number

_____

Applicant or Employee Signature   Date

REFUSAL OR REVOCATION OF CONSENT STATEMENT

(DO NOT SIGN UNLESS YOU HAVE DECIDED THAT YOU WILL NOT CONSENT, OR WILL NO LONGER CONSENT TO [INSERT COMPANY NAME] OBTAINING CONSUMER REPORTS OR INVESTIGATIVE CONSUMER REPORTS REGARDING YOU FOR EMPLOYMENT PURPOSES.)

I do not consent to [INSERT COMPANY NAME] obtaining consumer reports or investigative reports about me for employment purposes. If I have previously granted my consent, I hereby revoke it and understand that such revocation will take effect immediately after [INSERT COMPANY NAME] receives this written revocation and has actual knowledge of it sufficient to communicate the revocation to those employees or agents of [INSERT COMPANY NAME] who typically request consumer reports for [INSERT COMPANY NAME].

Name of Applicant or Employee (Printed)   Social Security Number

Applicant or Employee Signature   Date

Pre-Employment Legal Guidelines (California Model)

Consult a lawyer regarding the laws in your state.

Subject	Acceptable	Unacceptable
Name	• Name. • "Have you ever used another name?" Or "Is any additional information relative to change of name, use of an assumed name, or nickname necessary to enable a check on your work and education record? If yes, please explain."	• Maiden name.
Residence	• Place of residence.	• "Do you own or rent your home?"
Age	• Statement that hire is subject to verification that applicant meets legal age requirements. • "If hired, can you show proof of age?" • "Are you over eighteen?" • "If under eighteen, could you, after employment, submit a work permit?"	• Age. • Birth date. • Dates of attendance or completion of elementary or high school. • Questions that tend to identify applicants over age forty.

Subject	Acceptable	Unacceptable
Birthplace, Citizenship	• "Could you, after employment, submit verification of your legal right to work in the United States?" • Statement that such proof may be required after a decision is made to hire the candidate.	• Birthplace of applicant, applicant's parents, spouse, or other relatives. • "Are you a U.S. citizen?" or citizenship of applicant, applicant's parents, spouse, or other relatives. • Requirements that applicant produce naturalization, first papers, or alien card prior to a decision to hire.
National Origin	• Language applicant reads, speaks, or writes, if use of a language other than English is relevant to the job for which applicant is applying.	• Questions as to nationality, lineage, ancestry, national origin, descent, or parentage of applicant, applicant's parents, or spouse. • "What is your mother tongue?" • Language commonly used by applicant. • How applicant acquired ability to read, write, or speak a foreign language.

Subject	Acceptable	Unacceptable
Sex, Marital Status, Family	• Name and address of parent or guardian if applicant is a minor. • Statement of company policy regarding work assignment of employees who are related.	• Questions that indicate applicant's sex. • Questions that indicate applicant's marital status. • Number and/or ages of children or dependents. • Provisions for child care. • Questions regarding pregnancy, child bearing, or birth control. • Name and address of relative, spouse, or children of adult applicants.
Race Color		• Questions as to applicant's race or color. • Questions regarding applicant's complexion or color of skin, eyes, hair.

Subject	Acceptable	Unacceptable
Credit Report		• Any report that would indicate information that is otherwise illegal to ask; e.g., marital status, age, residency, etc.
Physical Description, Photograph	• Statement that photograph may be required after employment.	• Questions as to applicant's height and weight. • Require applicant to affix a photograph to application. • Request applicant, at his or her option, to submit a photograph. • Require a photograph after interview but before employment. • Videotaping interviews.

Subject	Acceptable	Unacceptable
Physical or Mental Disability	• Statement by employer that offer may be made contingent on an applicant passing a job-related physical examination. • "Can you perform (specific task)?"	• Questions regarding applicant's general medical condition, state of health, or illnesses. • Questions regarding receipt of Workers' Compensation. • "Do you have any physical or mental disabilities or handicaps?"
Religion	• Statement by employer of regular days, hours, or shifts to be worked.	• Questions regarding applicant's religion. • Religious days observed. • "Does your religion prevent you from working weekends or holidays?"
Criminal Record	• Job-related questions about convictions, except those convictions that have been sealed, expunged, or statutorily eradicated.	• Arrest record. • "Have you ever been arrested?"

Subject	Acceptable	Unacceptable
Military Service	• Questions regarding relevant skills acquired during applicant's U.S. military service.	• General questions regarding military service such as dates and type of discharge. • Questions regarding service in a foreign military.
Organizations Activities	• "Please list job-related organizations, clubs, societies, professional societies, or other associations to which you belong—you may omit those which indicate your race, religious creed, color, disability, marital status, national origin, ancestry, sex, or age."	• "List all organizations, clubs, and lodges to which you belong."

Subject	Acceptable	Unacceptable
References	• "By whom were you referred for a position here?" • Names of persons willing to provide professional and/or character references for applicant.	• Questions of applicant's former employers or acquaintances that elicit information specifying the applicant's race, color, religious creed, national origin, ancestry, physical or mental disability, medical condition, marital status, age, or sex.
Notice in Case of Emergency	• Name and address of person to be notified in case of accident or emergency.	• Name and address of relative to be notified in case of accident or emergency.

Ten Unusual Interview Experiences

A recent survey asked vice presidents and personnel directors of the nation's one hundred largest corporations for their most unusual experiences interviewing prospective employees. They included:

- A job applicant who challenged the interviewer to arm wrestle.

- A job candidate who said he had never finished high school because he was kidnapped and kept in a closet in Mexico.

- A balding candidate who excused himself and then returned wearing a full hairpiece.

- A candidate who wore headphones to the interview and, when asked to remove them, explained that she could listen to the interviewer and the music at the same time.

- A candidate who said she didn't have time for lunch and then started to eat a hamburger and fries in the interviewer's office.

- A clumsy candidate who fell and broke an arm during the interview.

- A candidate who interrupted the questioning to phone her therapist for advice.

- A candidate who dozed off during the interview.

- A candidate who refused to sit down and insisted on being interviewed standing up.

- A candidate who muttered, "Would it be a problem if I'm angry most of the time?"

Reprinted with permission from *Parade*, copyright © 1996.

Services

I suggest that you try these services on yourself. If satisfied, proceed to the next step. If not, for whatever reason, that's fine too.

Credit Services

Hire*Right*

215 W. Alameda Avenue

Burbank, CA 91502

Toll Free: (800) 820-9029

Fax: (818) 567-1215

E-mail: hireright@frasco.com

Similar services to McAward-Shaw. Call for current fee schedules.

I would start with McAward-Shaw or Hire*Right* before dealing directly with other credit services.

Investigative Services

McAward-Shaw Associates, Inc.

18 West 27th Street

New York, NY 10001

Phone: (212) 725-4747

Toll Free: (800) 989-3463

Fax: (212) 683-1324

E-mail: mcaward@aol.com

The company will verify educational background, employment records, auto and criminal records, as well as do a credit check. Call for current fee schedule.

Searchers Investigating Company, Inc.

Lee J. Beck, President

100 S. Sunrise Way, Suite 330

Palm Springs, CA 92262

Phone: (760) 324-0902

Toll Free: (800) 992-4274

Fax: (800) 669-0193 or (760) 770-9813

Costs are from $400 and up, depending on the services requested.

Charles Levenberg Private Investigations

1592 Union Street

San Francisco, CA 94123

Phone: (415) 775-6991

Fax: (415) 695-1970

Costs begin at about $75 per hour. Call for an estimate depending on the type of service requested.

Drug Testing

Psychemedics Corporation

Regional offices in Boston, Los Angeles, Chicago, Dallas, Atlanta, Las Vegas, and Fort Lauderdale.

Toll Free: (800) 522-7424

Ask for references in your area. Rates depend upon services requested.

Associated Pathologists Laboratories

Corporate Office

4230 Burnham Avenue, Suite 250

Las Vegas, NV 89119-5480

Phone: (702) 733-3785

Fax: (702) 733-0318 (call before faxing)

Ask for current clients and sample toxicology reports. Rates also depend on the type of "profile" requested.

Burrows Paper Corporation, Corroc Division

200 Shotwell Drive

Franklin, Ohio 45005

Attn: Dave Casullo

Phone: (513) 746-1933

Toll Free: (800) 732-1933

Fax: (513) 746-8515

E-mail: d.casullo@burline.com

Dave manages a division of Burrows Paper Corporation. They produce lightweight corrugated packaging for restaurants. Dave also leads 335 employees in a drug-free environment. Ask Dave about the drug-testing program he currently uses.

Handwriting Analysis

Insyte, Inc.

June Canoles

10351 South Blaney Avenue

Cupertino, CA 95014

Phone: (408) 252-9696

Fax: (408) 252-4848

E-mail: J96 write@aol.com

Costs run about $150 for a two-page evaluation. Call for current rates.

Behavioral Testing Services

Consulting Psychologists Press, Inc.

3803 E. Bayshore Road, P.O. Box 10096

Palo Alto, CA 94303

Phone: (650) 969-8901

Toll Free: (800) 624-1765

Fax: (650) 969-8608

E-mail: custserv@cpp-db.com

Web site: http://www.cpp-db.com

You'll need an authorized professional to obtain and administer the

Myers-Briggs Type Indicator. Call, write, or visit their Web site for details.

Management Performance Groups

8800 Roswell Road, Suite 100

Atlanta, GA 30350

Phone: (770) 587-1500

Fax: (770) 587-1717

Ask for the short version of the Style Analysis. Costs run about

$90–$150 per two-page evaluation.

Notes

page 6   "The best thing we can do for our competitors...":
David Pritchard, "Wired For Hiring: Microsoft's
Slick Recruiting Machine," *Fortune*,
February 5, 1996, p. 123.

page 7   "I thought it was a no-miss thing.": Tony Razzano, as
quoted in "49ers Will 'Razz' the NFL Draft," in the
San Francisco Chronicle, April 17, 1990, p. E2.

page 12   Microsoft gets about 12,000 resumes a month:
Pritchard, p. 3.

page 24   The Gallo story: Milo Shelly, personal communication
in 1997.

page 40   Cisco Systems' Web site...: Bill Buchard, "Hire Great
People Fast,"*Fast Company*, August–September,
1997, p. 138.

page 55   A recent recruiting booklet...:*Recruiting '95*
(San Francisco: Good Life Publications, 1995), p. 12.

page 55   "It was just so easy...": John R. Emshwitter, "How
Low-Key Style Let a Con Man Steal Millions from
Bosses," *Wall Street Journal*, December 4, 1995, p. 1.

page 58   "Every time I go against my gut...": Colleen Barrett,
"Airline Industry's Top-Ranked Woman Keeps
Southwest's Small-Fry Spirit Alive,"
Wall Street Journal, November 30, 1995, p. B1.

page 68   The salesmen who fidget: Carl Sewell and Paul B.
Brown, *Customers for Life* (New York: Doubleday
Currency, 1990).

page 72   United Electric Controls in Boston…: Harvard
               Business School Case #N9-697006.

page 73   Lexicon Branding story: Richard Halstead, "Talk About
               an Identity Crisis," *Independent Journal,* July 31,
               1997, p. E1.

page 82   Pan Pacific story: Sandy Beebe, personal communica-
               tion in 1997.

page 83   United #232 details: "Tragedy and Luck," *Newsweek,*
               July 31, 1989, pp. 18–21.

page 116   Handwriting example of George Soros and Donna
               Karan: *Four Seasons Hotels & Resort Magazine,*
               Fall/Winter, 1995, p. 66.

page 122   "Facts in themselves…": Richard Saul Wurman,
               Information Anxiety (New York: Bantam Books,
               1990), pp. 172–173.

page 130   Buddy Ryan story: Timothy W. Smith, *New York Times,*
               December 27, 1995, p. B11. Also see Tom
               Fitzgerald, *San Francisco Chronicle,* December 28,
               1995, p. E6.

page 131   Walter J. Marks story: Lori Olszewski, "Ex–Richmond
               Schools Chief May Lose Kansas City Job: Expenses,
               Medical Leave Questioned," *San Francisco
               Chronicle,* February 13, 1995, p. A17.

page 133   Credit stories: Leslie Seism, "A Bad Credit Record
               Can Get You Rejected for Auto Insurance," *Wall
               Street Journal,* November 6, 1995, p. 1. Also see

Notes

"Garbage In, Garbage Out," *Smart Money*, October, 1996, p. 115. An attorney adds, "Credit reports are permissible areas of inquiry as long as the report does not identify the applicant's protected characteristics. The need for the report must also be reasonably related to the job position. Because of serious privacy concerns, an employer should always obtain a release before obtaining such credit reports. In fact, in certain circumstances, it is required that notice be given to a candidate of a background check."

page 140–142   Phone references: format #1, Leon Farley & Associates; format #2, Charles "Red" Scott, written communication from Gary Rogers.

page 148   "If each of us hires people who are smaller than we are…": David Ogilvy, *Ogilvy on Advertising* (New York: Vintage Books, 1985), p. 47.

page 151   "I invest in people…": Arthur Rock as quoted by Michael Miller, "How One Man Helps High-Tech Prospects Get to the Big Leagues," *Wall Street Journal*, December, 1985, p.1.

page 157–158   The Doubletree and Quad Graphics stories: Peter Carbonara, "Hire for Attitudes, Train for Skill," *Fast Company, Special Collectors' Edition: The Greatest Hits,Volume 1*, 1997, pp. 64–71.

page 166   "I brainwash myself with a scene.": Anthony Hopkins, *Newsweek*, December 11, 1995, p. 72.

page 167   AT&T story and statistics: "For Whom Bell Tolls," *Newsweek*, January 15, 1996, pp. 44–45; "Disconnected," *Time*, January 15, 1996, pp. 44–51; "John Walter Call Home," *Newsweek*, November 4, 1996, p. 42; "A Crafter of Corporate Culture," *New York Times*, October 24, 1996, p. C-1.

page 167   There are 18,000 unfilled positions…: Bill Birchard, "Hire Great People Fast," *Fast Company*, August–September, 1997, p. 134.

page 168   "Hire and promote first…": Dee Hock as quoted by Mitchell Waldrop, "The Trillion Dollar Vision of Dee Hock," *Fast Company*, October/November, 1996, p. 79.

page 170   "What is good communication?…": Max DePree, *Leadership Is an Art* (New York: Dell, 1990), p. 103

page 184   "…no one achieves a house…": Allen Wheelis, *How People Change* (New York: Harper Colophon, 1975), p. 101.

page 187   Interview Questions: Courtesy of Peter R. Johnson, Larry Stupski, Alan Dachs, and Kirsty Melville, among others.

page 191   Word Pictures & Puzzles: For hundreds of right-brain puzzles, see also "Mindtrap: The Game That Will Challenge the Way You Think," New York: Pressman Toy Company.

Notes

page 196   Sample Legal Release Forms: Courtesy of Scott
            Rechtschaffen, a partner with the law firm of
            Littler Mendelson in San Francisco.

page 202   Pre-Employment Legal Guidelines (California Model):
            From the Department of Fair Employment and
            Housing, State of California (1993). Another
            attorney also adds, "A prospective employer is not
            permitted to make any pre-employment inquiry
            that elicits information identifying a person on a
            basis covered by the state or federal civil rights laws.
            That rule cannot be sidestepped by requesting a
            candidate to authorize the release of such
            information by others."

Index

Index

Index

Index

About the Author

Pierre Mornell is a psychiatrist who helps companies large and small, public and private, evaluate and select key people.

He received his BA degree from UCLA where he graduated Phi Beta Kappa and summa cum laude in English Literature. He received his MD degree from UC Medical School in San Francisco, then interned at the Los Angeles County General Hospital before doing a four-year psychiatric residency at the Langley Porter Institute.

Since 1985, Dr. Mornell has lectured in IBM's Advanced Management Seminar and International Executive Programs. He acted as the first Dean of the University Faculty for the Young Presidents' Organization. He has led day programs at the Stanford and Harvard business schools and has served as a consultant to the presidents of organizations as diverse as Intuit, Kinko's, Northern Telecom (Canada), American Golf Corporation, Hellman & Friedman, Young Presidents' Organization, World Presidents' Organization, Pentagram Design, The Institute for the Future, and the Art Center College of Design. He also speaks about executive evaluation and managing change at conferences worldwide.

Dr. Mornell has been married to his wife, Linda, for thirty-one years, and they have a son and two daughters. He lives in Marin County, north of San Francisco.

About the Designer and Illustrator

Kit Hinrichs is a principal in Pentagram Design, Inc., an international design consultancy.

After graduating from the Art Center College of Design, Los Angeles, Kit worked as a graphic designer in several New York design offices. In 1965 he formed his first partnership—Russell & Hinrichs. He co-founded Jonson, Pedersen, Hinrichs, and Shakery in 1976, and became a principal in Pentagram, San Francisco in 1986.

His accumulated design experience incorporates a wide range of projects—corporate identities, annual reports, Web sites, sales promotions, exhibits, and editorial design for clients such as AT&T, Sony, Time Warner, Monterey Bay Aquarium, Gymboree, Potlatch, Fox River Paper, Transamerica, United Airlines, and San Jose Museum of Art.

His work is part of the permanent collection of the Museums of Modern Art(New York and San Francisco) and the Library of Congress.

Regan Dunnick is a freelance illustrator and a full-time faculty member at his alma mater, the Ringling School of Art and Design.

Regan has exhibited nationally and internationally and has won numerous medals and awards in such major exhibitions as the United Nations Environmental Show, The Hiroshima Memorial Design Show (Japan), and the American Institute of Graphic Arts exhibition. His work is in the permanent collection of The Library of Congress.

Regan's clients include *Atlantic Monthly*, *Playboy*, *Rolling Stone*, the *Washington Post*, the *New York Times*, G.Q., and *Business Week*.

More Advance Praise for *Hiring Smart*

"Smart leaders know that their companies compete on the basis of their talent, and that their most important decisions are hiring decisions. **Hiring Smart** gives us practical, step-by-step advice on how to hire people who are right for you. Wisdom gushes from every concise, friendly chapter about hiring and human nature. Give this book to every manager in your company and keep it handy; you'll need it!"
—*John A. Davis, Senior Lecturer of Business Administration, Harvard Business School*

"Pierre Mornell's knowledge of the hiring process and the characteristics required of successful executives is exceptional. He was especially helpful with Kinko's senior management team at a very critical time in our transition from over 125 companies to one unified organization."
—*Paul Orfalea, Founder & Chairperson, Kinko's, Inc.*

"**Hiring Smart** is an exceedingly useful and user-friendly guide to the important task of hiring the right person. It's also a thoughtful, witty, and insightful look at hiring and how to do it better."
—*Vilma S. Martinez, Director, Shell Oil Company*

"Dr. Mornell gets it exactly right. Any entrepreneur—in fact, anyone at all who hires key personnel—will benefit by incorporating these clear and very readable steps toward **Hiring Smart.**"
—*Sandra Kurtzig, Founder, ASK Computer Systems, Chairman & CEO, E-benefits*

"In our business, people are intrinsic to the personality and style of our company. We believe that hiring the right individuals is the key to our success. Dr. Mornell's book can help anyone, at any level of management, approach this most critical process more thoughtfully and effectively."
—*Gordon Segal, Founder & CEO, Crate & Barrel*

"**Hiring Smart** is the most important work on selecting key personnel in over a decade. Essential reading for any executive or manager who must make the right decision the first time, every time."
—*Milo Shelly, Vice President, E. & J. Gallo Winery*

"The book will make you say, 'Why didn't we think of these strategies ourselves?' But like all simple ideas, they are extremely difficult to implement, especially in an organization. I'm going to keep **Hiring Smart** on my desk at all times. "
—*David G. Price, Chairman of the Board, American Golf Corporation*

"Contrary to what I thought early in my career, hiring good people doesn't come naturally, and it isn't easy. **Hiring Smart** gives us a clear, straightforward map through this potentially treacherous terrain. I wish I'd had it twenty-five years ago, but better late than never!"
—*David Brown, President, Art Center College of Design*

"I seriously doubt that any executive can read this book and not gain from it. Dr. Mornell outlines tips for hiring that will greatly decrease the chances of making costly mistakes."
—*Robert A. Ferchat, Chairman & CEO, Bell Mobility, Canada*

"**Hiring Smart** works. I wish I had this tool thirty years and 5,000 employees ago. It will become an important part of our hiring practices."
—*Fritz Grupe, Jr., Chairman & CEO, The Grupe Company*

"I always considered my hiring techniques to be clever and insightful. That is, until I read **Hiring Smart.** This book exposed a number of flaws I had developed over the years in the incredibly important process of relationship creation. It's never too late to teach an old dog new tricks."
—*Laurence B. Mindel, Chairman & CEO, Il Fornaio Corporation*

More Advance Praise for *Hiring Smart*

"We all know that finding the right people is the key to success—often, the whole ballgame. Pierre Mornell brings a disciplined and practical sensibility to the hiring process. As one who has both succeeded and failed at hiring smart, I found Dr. Mornell's message invaluable."
—*N. J. Nicholas, Jr., Co-CEO, Time Warner, 1990-92*

"Pierre Mornell has put the spotlight on the most important decision in any business—choosing who to put on your team. Anyone who doesn't follow his advice will inevitably pay a huge price in both time and money."
—*T. Gary Rogers, Chairman & CEO, Dreyer's Grand Ice Cream*

"The simple yet eloquent style of Dr. Mornell's writing makes the book very user-friendly. I shall keep **Hiring Smart** within reach of my desk."
—*Haile T. Debas, M.D., Chancellor, University of California, San Francisco*

"A vital book in an urgent area where most of us are weak and the stakes are so very high. **Hiring Smart** is a brisk three-hour read, including time for reflection. In elegant how-to style, this book delivers with deep heuristics and homilies. Reading it will change your approach to hiring. It has mine."
—*Robert Johansen, President & CEO, Institute for the Future*